MEDITERRANEAN COOKBOOK 2022

MANY DELICIOUS RECIPES TO SURPRISE YOUR FRIENDS

KEN LEVY

Table of Contents

Sea Bass in a Pocket 9

Creamy Smoked Salmon Pasta 11

Slow Cooker Greek Chicken 13

Chicken Gyros 15

Slow Cooker Chicken Cassoulet 17

Greek Style Turkey Roast 20

Garlic Chicken with Couscous 22

Chicken Karahi 24

Chicken Cacciatore with Orzo 26

Slow Cooked Daube Provencal 28

Osso Bucco 30

Slow Cooker Beef Bourguignon 32

Balsamic Beef 35

Veal Pot Roast 37

Mediterranean Rice and Sausage 39

Spanish Meatballs 40

Cauliflower Steaks with Olive Citrus Sauce 42

Pistachio Mint Pesto Pasta 44

Burst Cherry Tomato Sauce with Angel Hair Pasta 46

Baked Tofu with Sun-Dried Tomatoes and Artichokes 48

Baked Mediterranean Tempeh with Tomatoes and Garlic 50

Roasted Portobello Mushrooms with Kale and Red Onion 53

Ricotta, Basil, and Pistachio–Stuffed Zucchini 57

Farro with Roasted Tomatoes and Mushrooms 59

- Baked Orzo with Eggplant, Swiss Chard, and Mozzarella ... 62
- Barley Risotto with Tomatoes ... 64
- Chickpeas and Kale with Spicy Pomodoro Sauce ... 66
- Roasted Feta with Kale and Lemon Yogurt ... 68
- Roasted Eggplant and Chickpeas with Tomato Sauce ... 70
- Baked Falafel Sliders ... 72
- Portobello Caprese ... 74
- Mushroom and Cheese Stuffed Tomatoes ... 76
- Tabbouleh ... 78
- Spicy Broccoli Rabe And Artichoke Hearts ... 80
- Shakshuka ... 82
- Spanakopita ... 84
- Tagine ... 86
- Citrus Pistachios and Asparagus ... 88
- Tomato and Parsley Stuffed Eggplant ... 90
- Ratatouille ... 92
- Gemista ... 94
- Stuffed Cabbage Rolls ... 96
- Brussels Sprouts with Balsamic Glaze ... 98
- Spinach Salad with Citrus Vinaigrette ... 100
- Simple Celery and Orange Salad ... 101
- Fried Eggplant Rolls ... 103
- Roasted Veggies and Brown Rice Bowl ... 105
- Cauliflower Hash with Carrots ... 107
- Garlicky Zucchini Cubes with Mint ... 108
- Zucchini and Artichokes Bowl with Faro ... 109
- 5-Ingredient Zucchini Fritters ... 111

Garlic-Roasted Tomatoes and Olives	113
Goat Cheese and Garlic Crostini	115
Rosemary-Roasted Red Potatoes	116
Avocado Egg Scramble	117
Morning Tostadas	119
Parmesan Omelet	121
Watermelon Pizza	122
Savory Muffins	123
Morning Pizza with Sprouts	124
Banana Quinoa	126
Egg Casserole with Paprika	127
Cauliflower Fritters	129
Creamy Oatmeal with Figs	130
Baked Oatmeal with Cinnamon	131
Almond Chia Porridge	132
Cocoa Oatmeal	133
Cinnamon Roll Oats	134
Pumpkin Oatmeal with Spices	135
Stewed Cinnamon Apples with Dates	137
Spiced Poached Pears	138
Cranberry Applesauce	140
Blueberry Compote	142
Dried Fruit Compote	144
Chocolate Rice Pudding	145
Fruit Compote	146
Stuffed Apples	148
Cinnamon-Stewed Dried Plums with Greek Yogurt	150

Vanilla-Poached Apricots 151

Creamy Spiced Almond Milk 152

Poached Pears with Greek Yogurt and Pistachio 153

Peaches Poached in Rose Water 155

Brown Betty Apple Dessert 157

Blueberry Oat Crumble 159

Date and Walnut Cookies 161

Moroccan Stuffed Dates 163

Fig Cookies 164

Almond Cookies 166

Turkish Delight Cookies 167

Anise Cookies 169

Spanish Nougat 171

Spanish Crumble Cakes 172

Greek Honey Cookies 174

Cinnamon Butter Cookies 176

Best French Meringues 177

Cinnamon Palmier 178

Honey Sesame Cookies 179

Baked Apples 181

Pumpkin Baked with Dry Fruit 182

Banana Shake Bowls 183

Cold Lemon Squares 184

Blackberry and Apples Cobbler 185

Black Tea Cake 187

Green Tea and Vanilla Cream 188

Figs Pie 189

- Cherry Cream 190
- Strawberries Cream 191
- Apples and Plum Cake 192
- Cinnamon Chickpeas Cookies 193
- Cocoa Brownies 195
- Cardamom Almond Cream 196
- Banana Cinnamon Cupcakes 197
- Rhubarb and Apples Cream 198
- Almond Rice Dessert 199
- Mediterranean Baked Apples 200
- Chia Almond Butter Pudding 201
- Sweet Rice Pudding 202
- Creamy Yogurt Banana Bowls 203
- . Lemon Pear Compote 204
- Healthy & Quick Energy Bites 205
- Healthy Coconut Blueberry Balls 206
- Panna Cotta 208
- Turkish Kunefe 210
- Crema Catalana 212
- Spanish Dessert Turron 214
- Shrimp & Pasta 216
- Poached Cod 218

Sea Bass in a Pocket

Preparation Time : 10 minutes

Cooking Time : 25 minutes

Servings : 4

Difficulty Level : Average

Ingredients:

- 4 sea bass fillets
- 4 sliced garlic cloves
- 1 sliced celery stalk
- 1 sliced zucchini
- 1 c. halved cherry tomatoes halved
- 1 shallot, sliced
- 1 tsp. dried oregano
- Salt and pepper

Directions:

Mix the garlic, celery, zucchini, tomatoes, shallot, and oregano in a bowl. Add salt and pepper to taste. Take 4 sheets of baking paper and arrange them on your working surface. Spoon the vegetable mixture in the center of each sheet.

Top with a fish fillet then wrap the paper well so it resembles a pocket. Place the wrapped fish in a baking tray and cook in the preheated oven at 350 F/176 C for 15 minutes. Serve the fish warm and fresh.

Nutrition (for 100g): 149 Calories 2.8g Fat 5.2g Carbohydrates 25.2g Protein 696mg Sodium

Creamy Smoked Salmon Pasta

Preparation Time : 5 minutes

Cooking Time : 35 minutes

Servings : 4

Difficulty Level : Average

Ingredients:

- 2 tbsps. olive oil
- 2 chopped garlic cloves
- 1 shallot, chopped
- 4 oz. or 113 g chopped salmon, smoked
- 1 c. green peas
- 1 c. heavy cream
- Salt and pepper
- 1 pinch chili flakes
- 8 oz. or 230 g penne pasta
- 6 c. water

Directions:

Place skillet on medium-high heat and add oil. Add the garlic and shallot. Cook for 5 minutes or until softened. Add peas, salt, pepper, and chili flakes. Cook for 10 minutes

Add the salmon, and continue cooking for 5-7 minutes more. Add heavy cream, reduce heat and cook for an extra 5 minutes.

In the meantime, place a pan with water and salt to your taste on high heat as soon as it boils, add penne pasta and cook for 8-10 minutes or until softened Drain the pasta, add to the salmon sauce and serve

Nutrition (for 100g): 393 Calories 20.8g Fat 38g Carbohydrates 3g Protein 836mg Sodium

Slow Cooker Greek Chicken

Preparation Time : 20 minutes

Cooking Time : 3 hours

Servings : 4

Difficulty Level : Average

Ingredients:

- 1 tablespoon extra-virgin olive oil
- 2 pounds boneless, chicken breasts
- ½ tsp kosher salt
- ¼ tsp black pepper
- 1 (12-ounce) jar roasted red peppers
- 1 cup Kalamata olives
- 1 medium red onion, cut into chunks
- 3 tablespoons red wine vinegar
- 1 tablespoon minced garlic
- 1 teaspoon honey
- 1 teaspoon dried oregano
- 1 teaspoon dried thyme
- ½ cup feta cheese (optional, for serving)
- Chopped fresh herbs: any mix of basil, parsley, or thyme (optional, for serving)

Directions:

Brush slow cooker with nonstick cooking spray or olive oil. Cook the olive oil in a large skillet. Season both side of the chicken breasts. Once the oil is hot, add the chicken breasts and sear on both sides (about 3 minutes).

Once cooked, transfer it to the slow cooker. Add the red peppers, olives, and red onion to the chicken breasts. Try to place the vegetables around the chicken and not directly on top.

In a small bowl, mix the vinegar, garlic, honey, oregano, and thyme. Once combined, pour it over the chicken. Cook the chicken on low for 3 hours or until no longer pink in the middle. Serve with crumbled feta cheese and fresh herbs.

Nutrition (for 100g): 399 Calories 17g Fat 12g Carbohydrates 50g Protein 793mg Sodium

Chicken Gyros

Preparation Time : 10 minutes

Cooking Time : 4 hours

Servings : 4

Difficulty Level : Average

Ingredients:

- 2 lbs. boneless chicken breasts or chicken tenders
- Juice of one lemon
- 3 cloves garlic
- 2 teaspoons red wine vinegar
- 2–3 tablespoons olive oil
- ½ cup Greek yogurt
- 2 teaspoons dried oregano
- 2–4 teaspoons Greek seasoning
- ½ small red onion, chopped
- 2 tablespoons dill weed
- Tzatziki Sauce
- 1 cup plain Greek yogurt
- 1 tablespoon dill weed
- 1 small English cucumber, chopped
- Pinch of salt and pepper
- 1 teaspoon onion powder
- <u>For Toppings:</u>

- Tomatoes
- Chopped cucumbers
- Chopped red onion
- Diced feta cheese
- Crumbled pita bread

Directions:

Slice the chicken breasts into cubes and place in the slow cooker. Add the lemon juice, garlic, vinegar, olive oil, Greek yogurt, oregano, Greek seasoning, red onion, and dill to the slow cooker and stir to make sure everything is well combined.

Cook on low for 5-6 hours or on high for 2-3 hours. In the meantime, incorporate all ingredients for the tzatziki sauce and stir. When well mixed, put in the refrigerator until the chicken is done.

When the chicken has finished cooking, serve with pita bread and any or all of the toppings listed above.

Nutrition (for 100g): 317 Calories 7.4g Fat 36.1g Carbohydrates 28.6g Protein 476mg Sodium

Slow Cooker Chicken Cassoulet

Preparation Time : 10 minutes

Cooking Time : 20 minutes

Servings : 16

Difficulty Level : Average

Ingredients:

- 1 cup dry navy beans, soaked
- 8 bone-in skinless chicken thighs
- 1 Polish sausage, cooked and chopped into bite-sized pieces (optional)
- 1¼ cup tomato juice
- 1 (28-ounce) can halved tomatoes
- 1 tbsp Worcestershire sauce
- 1 tsp instant beef or chicken bouillon granules
- ½ tsp dried basil
- ½ teaspoon dried oregano
- ½ teaspoon paprika
- ½ cup chopped celery
- ½ cup chopped carrot
- ½ cup chopped onion

Directions:

Brush the slow cooker with olive oil or nonstick cooking spray. In a mixing bowl, stir together the tomato juice, tomatoes, Worcestershire sauce, beef bouillon, basil, oregano, and paprika. Make sure the ingredients are well combined.

Place the chicken and sausage into the slow cooker and cover with the tomato juice mixture. Top with celery, carrot, and onion. Cook on low for 10–12 hours.

Nutrition (for 100g): 244 Calories 7g Fat 25g Carbohydrates 21g

Slow Cooker Chicken Provencal

Preparation Time : 5 minutes

Cooking Time : 8 hours

Servings : 4

Difficulty Level : Easy

Ingredients:

- 4 (6-ounce) skinless bone-in chicken breast halves
- 2 teaspoons dried basil
- 1 teaspoon dried thyme
- 1/8 teaspoon salt
- 1/8 teaspoon freshly ground black pepper
- 1 yellow pepper, diced
- 1 red pepper, diced
- 1 (15.5-ounce) can cannellini beans
- 1 (14.5-ounce) can petite tomatoes with basil, garlic, and oregano, undrained

Directions:

Brush the slow cooker with nonstick olive oil. Add all the ingredients to the slow cooker and stir to combine. Cook on low for 8 hours.

Nutrition (for 100g): 304 Calories 4.5g Fat 27.3g Carbohydrates 39.4g Protein 639mg Sodium

Greek Style Turkey Roast

Preparation Time : 20 minutes

Cooking Time : 7 hours and 30 minutes

Servings : 8

Difficulty Level : Average

Ingredients:

- 1 (4-pound) boneless turkey breast, trimmed
- ½ cup chicken broth, divided
- 2 tablespoons fresh lemon juice
- 2 cups chopped onion
- ½ cup pitted Kalamata olives
- ½ cup oil-packed sun-dried tomatoes, thinly sliced
- 1 teaspoon Greek seasoning
- ½ teaspoon salt
- ¼ teaspoon fresh ground black pepper
- 3 tablespoons all-purpose flour (or whole wheat)

Directions:

Brush the slow cooker with nonstick cooking spray or olive oil. Add the turkey, ¼ cup of the chicken broth, lemon juice, onion, olives, sun-dried tomatoes, Greek seasoning, salt and pepper to the slow cooker.

Cook on low for 7 hours. Scourge the flour into the remaining ¼ cup of chicken broth, then stir gently into the slow cooker. Cook for an additional 30 minutes.

Nutrition (for 100g): 341 Calories 19g Fat 12g Carbohydrates 36.4g Protein 639mg Sodium

Garlic Chicken with Couscous

Preparation Time : 25 minutes

Cooking Time : 7 hours

Servings : 4

Difficulty Level : Average

Ingredients:

- 1 whole chicken, cut into pieces
- 1 tablespoon extra-virgin olive oil
- 6 cloves garlic, halved
- 1 cup dry white wine
- 1 cup couscous
- ½ teaspoon salt
- ½ teaspoon pepper
- 1 medium onion, thinly sliced
- 2 teaspoons dried thyme
- 1/3 cup whole wheat flour

Directions:

Cook the olive oil in a heavy skillet. When skillet is hot, add the chicken to sear. Make sure the chicken pieces don't touch each other. Cook with the skin side down for about 3 minutes or until browned.

Brush your slow cooker with nonstick cooking spray or olive oil. Put the onion, garlic, and thyme into the slow cooker and sprinkle with salt and pepper. Stir in the chicken on top of the onions.

In a separate bowl, whisk the flour into the wine until there are no lumps, then pour over the chicken. Cook on low for 7 hours or until done. You can cook on high for 3 hours as well. Serve the chicken over the cooked couscous and spoon sauce over the top.

Nutrition (for 100g): 440 Calories 17.5g Fat 14g Carbohydrates 35.8g Protein 674mg Sodium

Chicken Karahi

Preparation Time : 5 minutes

Cooking Time : 5 hours

Servings : 4

Difficulty Level : Easy

Ingredients:

- 2 lbs. chicken breasts or thighs
- ¼ cup olive oil
- 1 small can tomato paste
- 1 tablespoon butter
- 1 large onion, diced
- ½ cup plain Greek yogurt
- ½ cup water
- 2 tablespoons ginger in garlic paste
- 3 tablespoons fenugreek leaves
- 1 teaspoon ground coriander
- 1 medium tomato
- 1 teaspoon red chili
- 2 green chilies
- 1 teaspoon turmeric
- 1 tablespoon garam masala
- 1 teaspoon cumin powder
- 1 teaspoon sea salt
- ¼ teaspoon nutmeg

Directions:

Brush the slow cooker with nonstick cooking spray. In a small bowl, thoroughly mix all of the spices. Mix in the chicken to the slow cooker, followed by the ingredients' rest, including the spice mixture. Stir until everything is well mixed with the spices.

Cook on low for 4–5 hours. Serve with naan or Italian bread.

Nutrition (for 100g): 345 Calories 9.9g Fat 10g Carbohydrates 53.7g Protein 715mg Sodium

Chicken Cacciatore with Orzo

Preparation Time : 20 minutes

Cooking Time : 4 hours

Servings : 6

Difficulty Level : Easy

Ingredients:

- 2 pounds skin-on chicken thighs
- 1 tablespoon olive oil
- 1 cup mushrooms, quartered
- 3 carrots, chopped
- 1 small jar Kalamata olives
- 2 (14-ounce) cans diced tomatoes
- 1 small can tomato paste
- 1 cup red wine
- 5 garlic cloves
- 1 cup orzo

Directions:

In a large skillet, cook the olive oil. When the oil is heated, add the chicken, skin side down, and sear it. Make sure the pieces of chicken don't touch each other.

When the chicken is browned, add to the slow cooker along with all the ingredients except the orzo. Cook the chicken on low for 2 hours, then add the orzo and cook for an additional 2 hours. Serve with a crusty French bread.

Nutrition (for 100g): 424 Calories 16g Fat 10g Carbohydrates 11g Protein 845mg Sodium

Slow Cooked Daube Provencal

Preparation Time : 15 minutes

Cooking Time : 8 hours

Servings : 8

Difficulty Level : Average

Ingredients:

- 1 tablespoon olive oil
- 10 garlic cloves, minced
- 2 pounds boneless chuck roast
- 1½ teaspoons salt, divided
- ½ teaspoon freshly ground black pepper
- 1 cup dry red wine
- 2 cups carrots, chopped
- 1½ cups onion, chopped
- ½ cup beef broth
- 1 (14-ounce) can diced tomatoes
- 1 tablespoon tomato paste
- **1 teaspoon fresh rosemary, chopped**
- 1 teaspoon fresh thyme, chopped
- ½ teaspoon orange zest, grated
- ½ teaspoon ground cinnamon
- ¼ teaspoon ground cloves
- 1 bay leaf

Directions:

Preheat a skillet and then add the olive oil. Add the minced garlic and onions and cook until the onions are soft and the garlic begins to brown.

Add the cubed meat, salt, and pepper and cook until the meat has browned. Transfer the meat to the slow cooker. Mix in the beef broth to the skillet and let simmer for about 3 minutes to deglaze the pan, then pour into slow cooker over the meat.

Incorporate the rest of the ingredients to the slow cooker and stir well to combine. Adjust slow cooker to low and cook for 8 hours, or set to high and cook for 4 hours. Serve with a side of egg noodles, rice or some crusty Italian bread.

Nutrition (for 100g): 547 Calories 30.5g Fat 22g Carbohydrates 45.2g Protein 809mg Sodium

Osso Bucco

Preparation Time : 30 minutes

Cooking Time : 8 hours

Servings : 3

Difficulty Level : Average

Ingredients:

- 4 beef shanks or veal shanks
- 1 teaspoon sea salt
- ½ teaspoon ground black pepper
- 3 tablespoons whole wheat flour
- 1–2 tablespoons olive oil
- 2 medium onions, diced
- 2 medium carrots, diced
- 2 celery stalks, diced
- 4 garlic cloves, minced
- 1 (14-ounce) can diced tomatoes
- 2 teaspoons dried thyme leaves
- ½ cup beef or vegetable stock

Directions:

Season the shanks on both sides, then dip in the flour to coat. Heat a large skillet over high heat. Add the olive oil. Once the oil is hot, add the shanks and brown evenly on both sides. When browned, transfer to the slow cooker.

Pour the stock into the skillet and let simmer for 3–5 minutes while stirring to deglaze the pan. Transfer the rest of the ingredients to the slow cooker and pour the stock from the skillet over the top.

Adjust the slow cooker to low and cook for 8 hours. Serve the Osso Bucco over quinoa, brown rice, or even cauliflower rice.

Nutrition (for 100g): 589 Calories 21.3g Fat 15g Carbohydrates 74.7g Protein 893mg Sodium

Slow Cooker Beef Bourguignon

Preparation Time : 5 minutes

Cooking Time : 8 hours

Servings : 8

Difficulty Level : Difficult

Ingredients:

- 1 tablespoon extra-virgin olive oil
- 6 ounces bacon, roughly chopped
- 3 pounds beef brisket, trimmed of fat, cut into 2-inch cubes
- 1 large carrot, sliced
- 1 large white onion, diced
- 6 cloves garlic, minced and divided
- ½ teaspoon coarse salt
- ½ teaspoon freshly ground pepper
- 2 tablespoons whole wheat
- 12 small pearl onions
- 3 cups red wine (Merlot, Pinot Noir, or Chianti)
- 2 cups beef stock
- 2 tablespoons tomato paste
- 1 beef bouillon cube, crushed
- 1 teaspoon fresh thyme, finely chopped
- 2 tablespoons fresh parsley
- 2 bay leaves
- 2 tablespoons butter or 1 tablespoon olive oil

- 1 pound fresh small white or brown mushrooms, quartered

Directions:

Heat up a skillet over medium-high heat, then add the olive oil. When the oil has heated, cook the bacon until it is crisp, then place it in your slow cooker. Save the bacon fat in the skillet.

Pat dry the beef and cook it in the same skillet with the bacon fat until all sides have the same brown coloring. Transfer to the slow cooker.

Mix in the onions and carrots to the slow cooker and season with the salt and pepper. Stir to combine the ingredients and make sure everything is seasoned.

Stir in the red wine into the skillet and simmer for 4–5 minutes to deglaze the pan, then whisk in the flour, stirring until smooth. Continue cooking until the liquid reduces and thickens a bit.

When the liquid has thickened, pour it into the slow cooker and stir to coat everything with the wine mixture. Add the tomato paste, bouillon cube, thyme, parsley, 4 cloves of garlic, and bay leaf. Adjust your slow cooker to high and cook for 6 hours, or set to low and cook for 8 hours.

Soften the butter or heat the olive oil in a skillet over medium heat. When the oil is hot, stir in the remaining 2 cloves of garlic and cook for about 1 minute before adding the mushrooms. Cook the mushrooms until soft, then add to the slow cooker and mix to combine.

Serve with mashed potatoes, rice or noodles.

Nutrition (for 100g): 672 Calories 32g Fat 15g Carbohydrates 56g Protein 693mg Sodium

Balsamic Beef

Preparation Time : 5 minutes

Cooking Time : 8 hours

Servings : 10

Difficulty Level : Average

Ingredients:

- 2 pounds boneless chuck roast
- 1 tablespoon olive oil
- Rub
- 1 teaspoon garlic powder
- ½ teaspoon onion powder
- 1 teaspoon sea salt
- ½ teaspoon freshly ground black pepper
- Sauce
- ½ cup balsamic vinegar
- 2 tablespoons honey
- 1 tablespoon honey mustard
- 1 cup beef broth
- 1 tablespoon tapioca, whole wheat flour, or cornstarch (to thicken sauce when it is done cooking if desired)

Directions:

Incorporate all of the ingredients for the rub.

In a separate bowl, mix the balsamic vinegar, honey, honey mustard, and beef broth. Coat the roast in olive oil, then rub in the spices from the rub mix. Place the roast in the slow cooker and then pour the sauce over the top. Adjust the slow cooker to low and cook for 8 hours.

If you want to thicken the sauce when the roast is done cooking transfer it from the slow cooker to a serving plate. Then fill the liquid into a saucepan and heat to boiling on the stovetop. Mix the flour until smooth and let simmer until the sauce thickens.

Nutrition (for 100g): 306 Calories 19g Fat 13g Carbohydrates 25g Protein 823mg Sodium

Veal Pot Roast

Preparation Time : 20 minutes

Cooking Time : 5 hours

Servings : 8

Difficulty Level : Average

Ingredients:

- 2 tablespoons olive oil
- Salt and pepper
- 3-pound boneless veal roast, tied
- 4 medium carrots, peeled
- 2 parsnips, peeled and halved
- 2 white turnips, peeled and quartered
- 10 garlic cloves, peeled
- 2 sprigs fresh thyme
- 1 orange, scrubbed and zested
- 1 cup chicken or veal stock

Directions:

Heat a large skillet over medium-high heat. Scour veal roast all over with olive oil, then season with salt and pepper. When the skillet is hot, add the veal roast and sear on all sides. This will take about 3 minutes on every side, but this process seals in the juices and makes the meat succulent.

When cooked, place it to the slow cooker. Toss the carrots, parsnips, turnips, and garlic into the skillet. Stir and cook for about 5 minutes—not all the way through, just to get some of the brown bits from the veal and give them a bit of color.

Transfer the vegetables to the slow cooker, placing them all around the meat. Top the roast with the thyme and the zest from the orange. Cut the orange in half and squeeze the juice over the top of the meat. Add the chicken stock, then cook the roast on low for 5 hours.

Nutrition (for 100g): 426 Calories 12.8g Fat 10g Carbohydrates 48.8g Protein 822mg Sodium

Mediterranean Rice and Sausage

Preparation Time : 15 minutes

Cooking Time : 8 hours

Servings : 6

Difficulty Level : Average

Ingredients:

- 1½ pounds Italian sausage, crumbled
- 1 medium onion, chopped
- 2 tablespoons steak sauce
- 2 cups long grain rice, uncooked
- 1 (14-ounce) can diced tomatoes with juice
- ½ cup water
- 1 medium green pepper, diced

Directions:

Spray your slow cooker with olive oil or nonstick cooking spray. Add the sausage, onion, and steak sauce to the slow cooker. Set on low for 8 to 10 hours.

After 8 hours, add the rice, tomatoes, water and green pepper. Stir to combine thoroughly. Cook an additional 20 to 25 minutes.

Nutrition (for 100g): 650 Calories 36g Fat 11g Carbohydrates 22g Protein 633mg Sodium

Spanish Meatballs

Preparation Time : 20 minutes

Cooking Time : 5 hours

Servings : 6

Difficulty Level : Difficult

Ingredients:

- 1-pound ground turkey
- 1-pound ground pork
- 2 eggs
- 1 (20-ounce) can diced tomatoes
- ¾ cup sweet onion, minced, divided
- ¼ cup plus 1 tablespoon breadcrumbs
- 3 tablespoons fresh parsley, chopped
- 1½ teaspoons cumin
- 1½ teaspoons paprika (sweet or hot)

Directions:

Spray the slow cooker with olive oil.

In a mixing bowl, incorporate the ground meat, eggs, about half of the onions, the breadcrumbs, and the spices.

Wash your hands and mix together until everything is well combined. Do not over-mix, though, as this makes for tough meatballs. Shape into meatballs. How big you make them will obviously determine how many total meatballs you get.

In a skillet, cook 2 tablespoons of olive oil over medium heat. Once hot, mix in the meatballs and brown on all sides. Make sure the balls aren't touching each other so they brown evenly. Once done, transfer them to the slow cooker.

Add the rest of the onions and the tomatoes to the skillet and allow them to cook for a few minutes, scraping the brown bits from the meatballs up to add flavor. Transfer the tomatoes over the meatballs in the slow cooker and cook on low for 5 hours.

Nutrition (for 100g): 372 Calories 21.7g Fat 15g Carbohydrates 28.6 Protein 772mg Sodium

Cauliflower Steaks with Olive Citrus Sauce

Preparation Time : 15 minutes

Cooking Time : 30 minutes

Servings : 4

Difficulty Level : Average

Ingredients:

- 1 or 2 large heads cauliflower
- 1/3 cup extra-virgin olive oil
- ¼ teaspoon kosher salt
- 1/8 teaspoon ground black pepper
- Juice of 1 orange
- Zest of 1 orange
- ¼ cup black olives, pitted and chopped
- 1 tablespoon Dijon or grainy mustard
- 1 tablespoon red wine vinegar
- ½ teaspoon ground coriander

Directions:

Preheat the oven to 400°F. Put parchment paper or foil into the baking sheet. Cut off the stem of the cauliflower so it will sit upright. Slice it vertically into four thick slabs. Place the cauliflower on the prepared baking sheet. Dash with the olive oil, salt, and black pepper. Bake for about 30 minutes.

In a medium bowl, stir the orange juice, orange zest, olives, mustard, vinegar, and coriander; mix well. Serve with the sauce.

Nutrition (for 100g): 265 Calories 21g Fat 4g Carbohydrates 5g Protein 693mg Sodium

Pistachio Mint Pesto Pasta

Preparation Time : 10 minutes

Cooking Time : 10 minutes

Servings : 4

Difficulty Level : Average

Ingredients:

- 8 ounces whole-wheat pasta
- 1 cup fresh mint
- ½ cup fresh basil
- 1/3 cup unsalted pistachios, shelled
- 1 garlic clove, peeled
- ½ teaspoon kosher salt
- Juice of ½ lime
- 1/3 cup extra-virgin olive oil

Directions:

Cook the pasta following the package directions. Drain, reserving ½ cup of the pasta water, and set aside. In a food processor, add the mint, basil, pistachios, garlic, salt, and lime juice. Process until the pistachios are coarsely ground. Stir in the olive oil in a slow, steady stream and process until incorporated.

In a large bowl, incorporate the pasta with the pistachio pesto. If a thinner, more saucy consistency is desired, add some of the reserved pasta water and toss well.

Nutrition (for 100g): 420 Calories 3g Fat 2g Carbohydrates 11g Protein 593mg Sodium

Burst Cherry Tomato Sauce with Angel Hair Pasta

Preparation Time : 10 minutes

Cooking Time : 20 minutes

Servings : 4

Difficulty Level : Average

Ingredients:

- 8 ounces angel hair pasta
- 2 tablespoons extra-virgin olive oil
- 3 garlic cloves, minced
- 3 pints cherry tomatoes
- ½ teaspoon kosher salt
- ¼ teaspoon red pepper flakes
- ¾ cup fresh basil, chopped
- 1 tablespoon white balsamic vinegar (optional)
- ¼ cup grated Parmesan cheese (optional)

Directions:

Cook the pasta following the package directions. Drain and set aside.

Cook the olive oil in a skillet or large sauté pan over medium-high heat. Stir in the garlic and sauté for 30 seconds. Mix in the tomatoes, salt, and red pepper flakes and cook, stirring occasionally, until the tomatoes burst, about 15 minutes.

Take out from the heat and stir in the pasta and basil. Toss together well. (For out-of-season tomatoes, add the vinegar, if desired, and mix well.) Serve.

Nutrition (for 100g): 305 Calories 8g Fat 3g Carbohydrates 11g Protein 559mg Sodium

Baked Tofu with Sun-Dried Tomatoes and Artichokes

Preparation Time : 30 minutes
Cooking Time : 30 minutes
Servings : 4
Difficulty Level : Average

Ingredients:

- 1 (16-ounce) package extra-firm tofu, cut into 1-inch cubes
- 2 tablespoons extra-virgin olive oil, divided
- 2 tablespoons lemon juice, divided
- 1 tablespoon low-sodium soy sauce
- 1 onion, diced
- ½ teaspoon kosher salt
- 2 garlic cloves, minced
- 1 (14-ounce) can artichoke hearts, drained
- 8 sun-dried tomato
- ¼ teaspoon freshly ground black pepper
- 1 tablespoon white wine vinegar
- Zest of 1 lemon
- ¼ cup fresh parsley, chopped

Directions:

Prepare the oven to 400°F. Position the foil or parchment paper into the baking sheet. In a bowl, combine the tofu, 1 tablespoon of the olive oil, 1 tablespoon of the lemon juice, and the soy sauce. Set aside and marinate for 15 to 30 minutes. Arrange the tofu in a single layer on the prepared baking sheet and bake for 20 minutes, turning once, until light golden brown.

Cook the remaining 1 tablespoon olive oil in a large skillet or sauté pan over medium heat. Add the onion and salt; sauté until translucent, 5 to 6 minutes. Mix in the garlic and sauté for 30 seconds. Then put the artichoke hearts, sun-dried tomatoes, and black pepper and sauté for 5 minutes. Add the white wine vinegar and the remaining 1 tablespoon lemon juice and deglaze the pan, scraping up any brown bits. Take the pan from the heat and put in the lemon zest and parsley. Gently mix in the baked tofu.

Nutrition (for 100g): 230 Calories 14g Fat 5g Carbohydrates 14g Protein 593mg Sodium

Baked Mediterranean Tempeh with Tomatoes and Garlic

Preparation Time : 25 minutes, plus 4 hours to marinate

Cooking Time : 35 minutes

Servings : 4

Difficulty Level : Difficult

Ingredients:

- <u>For the Tempeh</u>
- 12 ounces tempeh
- ¼ cup white wine
- 2 tablespoons extra-virgin olive oil
- 2 tablespoons lemon juice
- Zest of 1 lemon
- ¼ teaspoon kosher salt
- ¼ teaspoon freshly ground black pepper
- <u>For the Tomatoes and Garlic Sauce</u>
- 1 tablespoon extra-virgin olive oil
- 1 onion, diced
- 3 garlic cloves, minced
- 1 (14.5-ounce) can no-salt-added crushed tomatoes
- 1 beefsteak tomato, diced
- 1 dried bay leaf
- 1 teaspoon white wine vinegar

- 1 teaspoon lemon juice
- 1 teaspoon dried oregano
- 1 teaspoon dried thyme
- ¾ teaspoon kosher salt
- ¼ cup basil, cut into ribbons

Directions:

To Make the Tempeh

Place the tempeh in a medium saucepan. Fill enough water to cover it by 1 to 2 inches. Bring to a boil over medium-high heat, cover, and lower heat to a simmer. Cook for 10 to 15 minutes. Remove the tempeh, pat dry, cool, and cut into 1-inch cubes.

Mix the white wine, olive oil, lemon juice, lemon zest, salt, and black pepper. Add the tempeh, cover the bowl, put in the refrigerator for 4 hours, or overnight. Preheat the oven to 375°F. Place the marinated tempeh and the marinade in a baking dish and cook for 15 minutes.

To Make the Tomatoes and Garlic Sauce

Cook the olive oil in a large skillet over medium heat. Add the onion and sauté until transparent, 3 to 5 minutes. Mix in the garlic and sauté for 30 seconds. Add the crushed tomatoes, beefsteak tomato, bay leaf, vinegar, lemon juice, oregano, thyme, and salt. Mix well. Simmer for 15 minutes.

Add the baked tempeh to the tomato mixture and gently mix together. Garnish with the basil.

SUBSTITUTION TIP: If you're out of tempeh or simply want to speed up the cooking process, you can swap in a 14.5-ounce can of white beans for the tempeh. Rinse the beans and put them to the sauce with the crushed tomatoes. It still makes a great vegan entrée in half the time!

Nutrition (for 100g): 330 Calories 20g Fat 4g Carbohydrates 18g Protein 693mg Sodium

Roasted Portobello Mushrooms with Kale and Red Onion

Preparation Time : 30 minutes

Cooking Time : 30 minutes

Servings : 4

Difficulty Level : Difficult

Ingredients:

- ¼ cup white wine vinegar
- 3 tablespoons extra-virgin olive oil, divided
- ½ teaspoon honey
- ¾ teaspoon kosher salt, divided
- ¼ teaspoon freshly ground black pepper
- 4 large portobello mushrooms, stems removed
- 1 red onion, julienned
- 2 garlic cloves, minced
- 1 (8-ounce) bunch kale, stemmed and chopped small
- ¼ teaspoon red pepper flakes
- ¼ cup grated Parmesan or Romano cheese

Directions:

Situate parchment paper or foil into the baking sheet. In a medium bowl, whisk together the vinegar, 1½ tablespoons of the olive oil, honey, ¼ teaspoon of the salt, and the black pepper. Lay the mushrooms on the baking sheet and pour the marinade over them. Marinate for 15 to 30 minutes.

Meanwhile, preheat the oven to 400°F. Bake the mushrooms for 20 minutes, turning over halfway through. Heat the remaining 1½ tablespoons olive oil in a large skillet or ovenproof sauté pan over medium-high heat. Add the onion and the remaining ½ teaspoon salt and sauté until golden brown, 5 to 6 minutes. Mix in the garlic and sauté for 30 seconds. Mix in the kale and red pepper flakes and sauté until the kale cooks down, about 5 minutes.

Remove the mushrooms from the oven and increase the temperature to broil. Carefully pour the liquid from the baking sheet into the pan with the kale mixture; mix well. Turn the mushrooms over so that the stem side is facing up. Spoon some of the kale mixture on top of each mushroom. Sprinkle 1 tablespoon Parmesan cheese on top of each. Broil until golden brown.

Nutrition (For 100g): 200 Calories 13g Fat 4g Carbohydrates 8g Protein

Balsamic Marinated Tofu with Basil and Oregano

Preparation Time : 40 minutes

Cooking Time : 30 minutes

Servings : 4

Difficulty Level : Average

Ingredients:

- ¼ cup extra-virgin olive oil
- ¼ cup balsamic vinegar
- 2 tablespoons low-sodium soy sauce
- 3 garlic cloves, grated
- 2 teaspoons pure maple syrup
- Zest of 1 lemon
- 1 teaspoon dried basil
- 1 teaspoon dried oregano
- ½ teaspoon dried thyme
- ½ teaspoon dried sage
- ¼ teaspoon kosher salt
- ¼ teaspoon freshly ground black pepper
- ¼ teaspoon red pepper flakes (optional)
- 1 (16-ounce) block extra firm tofu

Directions:

In a bowl or gallon zip-top bag, mix together the olive oil, vinegar, soy sauce, garlic, maple syrup, lemon zest, basil, oregano, thyme, sage, salt, black pepper, and red pepper flakes, if desired. Add the tofu and mix gently. Put in the refrigerator and marinate for 30 minutes, or up to overnight if you desire.

Prepare the oven to 425°F. Place parchment paper or foil into the baking sheet. Arrange the marinated tofu in a single layer on the prepared baking sheet. Bake for 20 to 30 minutes, flip over halfway through, until slightly crispy.

Nutrition (for 100g): 225 Calories 16g Fat 2g Carbohydrates 13g Protein 493mg Sodium

Ricotta, Basil, and Pistachio-Stuffed Zucchini

Preparation Time : 15 minutes
Cooking Time : 25 minutes
Servings : 4
Difficulty Level : Average

Ingredients:

- 2 medium zucchinis, halved lengthwise
- 1 tablespoon extra-virgin olive oil
- 1 onion, diced
- 1 teaspoon kosher salt
- 2 garlic cloves, minced
- ¾ cup ricotta cheese
- ¼ cup unsalted pistachios, shelled and chopped
- ¼ cup fresh basil, chopped
- 1 large egg, beaten
- ¼ teaspoon freshly ground black pepper

Directions:

Ready the oven to 425°F. Situate parchment paper or foil into the baking sheet. Scoop out the seeds/pulp from the zucchini, leaving ¼-inch flesh around the edges. Situate the pulp to a cutting board and chop off the pulp.

Cook the olive oil in a sauté pan over medium heat. Add the onion, pulp, and salt and sauté about 5 minutes. Add the garlic and sauté 30 seconds. Mix the ricotta cheese, pistachios, basil, egg, and black pepper. Add the onion mixture and mix well.

Place the 4 zucchini halves on the prepared baking sheet. Spread the zucchini halves with the ricotta mixture. Bake until golden brown.

Nutrition (for 100g): 200 Calories 12g Fat 3g Carbohydrates 11g Protein 836mg Sodium

Farro with Roasted Tomatoes and Mushrooms

Preparation Time : 20 minutes
Cooking Time : 1 hour
Servings : 4
Difficulty Level : Difficult

Ingredients:

- <u>For the Tomatoes</u>
- 2 pints cherry tomatoes
- 1 teaspoon extra-virgin olive oil
- ¼ teaspoon kosher salt
- <u>For the Farro</u>
- 3 to 4 cups water
- ½ cup farro
- ¼ teaspoon kosher salt
- <u>For the Mushrooms</u>
- 2 tablespoons extra-virgin olive oil
- 1 onion, julienned
- ½ teaspoon kosher salt
- ¼ teaspoon freshly ground black pepper
- 10 ounces baby bell mushrooms, stemmed and sliced thin
- ½ cup no-salt-added vegetable stock

- 1 (15-ounce) can low-sodium cannellini beans, drained and rinsed
- 1 cup baby spinach
- 2 tablespoons fresh basil, cut into ribbons
- ¼ cup pine nuts, toasted
- Aged balsamic vinegar (optional)

Directions:

To Make the Tomatoes

Preheat the oven to 400°F. Put parchment paper or foil into the baking sheet. Mix the tomatoes, olive oil, and salt together on the baking sheet and roast for 30 minutes.

To Make the Farro

Bring the water, farro, and salt to a boil in a medium saucepan or pot over high heat. Allow to simmer, and cook for 30 minutes, or until the farro is al dente. Drain and set aside.

To Make the Mushrooms

Cook the olive oil in a large skillet or sauté pan over medium-low heat. Add the onions, salt, and black pepper and sauté until golden brown and starting to caramelize, about 15 minutes. Stir in the mushrooms, increase the heat to medium, and sauté until the liquid has evaporated and the mushrooms brown, about 10 minutes. Stir in the vegetable stock and deglaze the pan, scraping up any brown bits, and reduce the liquid for about 5 minutes. Add the beans and warm through, about 3 minutes.

Remove and stir in the spinach, basil, pine nuts, roasted tomatoes, and farro. Dash with balsamic vinegar, if desired.

Nutrition (for 100g): 375 Calories 15g Fat 10g Carbohydrates 14g Protein 769mg Sodium

Baked Orzo with Eggplant, Swiss Chard, and Mozzarella

Preparation Time : 20 minutes
Cooking Time : 60 minutes
Servings : 4
Difficulty Level : Average

Ingredients:

- 2 tablespoons extra-virgin olive oil
- 1 large (1-pound) eggplant, diced small
- 2 carrots, peeled and diced small
- 2 celery stalks, diced small
- 1 onion, diced small
- ½ teaspoon kosher salt
- 3 garlic cloves, minced
- ¼ teaspoon freshly ground black pepper
- 1 cup whole-wheat orzo
- 1 teaspoon no-salt-added tomato paste
- 1½ cups no-salt-added vegetable stock
- 1 cup Swiss chard, stemmed and chopped small
- 2 tablespoons fresh oregano, chopped
- Zest of 1 lemon
- 4 ounces mozzarella cheese, diced small
- ¼ cup grated Parmesan cheese
- 2 tomatoes, sliced ½-inch-thick

Directions:

Preheat the oven to 400°F. Cook the olive oil in a large oven-safe sauté pan over medium heat. Add the eggplant, carrots, celery, onion, and salt and sauté about 10 minutes. Add the garlic and black pepper and sauté about 30 seconds. Add the orzo and tomato paste and sauté 1 minute. Mix in the vegetable stock and deglaze the pan, scraping up the brown bits. Add the Swiss chard, oregano, and lemon zest and stir until the chard wilts.

Pull out and put in the mozzarella cheese. Smooth the top of the orzo mixture flat. Sprinkle the Parmesan cheese over the top. Spread the tomatoes in a single layer on top of the Parmesan cheese. Bake for 45 minutes.

Nutrition (for 100g): 470 Calories 17g Fat 7g Carbohydrates 18g Protein 769mg Sodium

Barley Risotto with Tomatoes

Preparation Time : 20 minutes

Cooking Time : 45 minutes

Servings : 4

Difficulty Level : Average

Ingredients:

- 2 tablespoons extra-virgin olive oil
- 2 celery stalks, diced
- ½ cup shallots, diced
- 4 garlic cloves, minced
- 3 cups no-salt-added vegetable stock
- 1 (14.5-ounce) can no-salt-added diced tomatoes
- 1 (14.5-ounce) can no-salt-added crushed tomatoes
- 1 cup pearl barley
- Zest of 1 lemon
- 1 teaspoon kosher salt
- ½ teaspoon smoked paprika
- ¼ teaspoon red pepper flakes
- ¼ teaspoon freshly ground black pepper
- 4 thyme sprigs
- 1 dried bay leaf
- 2 cups baby spinach
- ½ cup crumbled feta cheese
- 1 tablespoon fresh oregano, chopped

- 1 tablespoon fennel seeds, toasted (optional)

Directions:

Cook the olive oil in a large saucepan over medium heat. Add the celery and shallots and sauté, about 4 to 5 minutes. Add the garlic and sauté 30 seconds. Add the vegetable stock, diced tomatoes, crushed tomatoes, barley, lemon zest, salt, paprika, red pepper flakes, black pepper, thyme, and the bay leaf, and mix well. Let it boil, then lower to low, and simmer. Cook, stirring occasionally, for 40 minutes.

Remove the bay leaf and thyme sprigs. Stir in the spinach. In a small bowl, combine the feta, oregano, and fennel seeds. Serve the barley risotto in bowls topped with the feta mixture.

Nutrition (for 100g): 375 Calories 12g Fat 13g Carbohydrates 11g Protein 799mg Sodium

Chickpeas and Kale with Spicy Pomodoro Sauce

Preparation Time : 10 minutes
Cooking Time : 35 minutes
Servings : 4
Difficulty Level : Easy

Ingredients:

- 2 tablespoons extra-virgin olive oil
- 4 garlic cloves, sliced
- 1 teaspoon red pepper flakes
- 1 (28-ounce) can no-salt-added crushed tomatoes
- 1 teaspoon kosher salt
- ½ teaspoon honey
- 1 bunch kale, stemmed and chopped
- 2 (15-ounce) cans low-sodium chickpeas, drained and rinsed
- ¼ cup fresh basil, chopped
- ¼ cup grated pecorino Romano cheese

Directions:

Cook the olive oil in a sauté pan over medium heat. Stir in the garlic and red pepper flakes and sauté until the garlic is a light golden brown, about 2 minutes. Add the tomatoes, salt, and honey and mix well. Reduce the heat to low and simmer for 20 minutes.

Add the kale and mix in well. Cook about 5 minutes. Add the chickpeas and simmer about 5 minutes. Remove from heat and stir in the basil. Serve topped with pecorino cheese.

Nutrition (for 100g): 420 Calories 13g Fat 12g Carbohydrates 20g Protein 882mg Sodium

Roasted Feta with Kale and Lemon Yogurt

Preparation Time : 15 minutes

Cooking Time : 20 minutes

Servings : 4

Difficulty Level : Average

Ingredients:

- 1 tablespoon extra-virgin olive oil
- 1 onion, julienned
- ¼ teaspoon kosher salt
- 1 teaspoon ground turmeric
- ½ teaspoon ground cumin
- ½ teaspoon ground coriander
- ¼ teaspoon freshly ground black pepper
- 1 bunch kale, stemmed and chopped
- 7-ounce block feta cheese, cut into ¼-inch-thick slices
- ½ cup plain Greek yogurt
- 1 tablespoon lemon juice

Directions:

Preheat the oven to 400°F. Fry the olive oil in a large ovenproof skillet or sauté pan over medium heat. Add the onion and salt; sauté until lightly golden brown, about 5 minutes. Add the turmeric, cumin, coriander, and black pepper; sauté for 30 seconds. Add the kale and sauté about 2 minutes. Add ½ cup water and continue to cook down the kale, about 3 minutes.

Remove from the heat and place the feta cheese slices on top of the kale mixture. Introduce in the oven and bake until the feta softens, 10 to 12 minutes. In a small bowl, combine the yogurt and lemon juice. Serve the kale and feta cheese topped with the lemon yogurt.

Nutrition (for 100g): 210 Calories 14g Fat 2g Carbohydrates 11g Protein 836mg Sodium

Roasted Eggplant and Chickpeas with Tomato Sauce

Preparation Time : 15 minutes
Cooking Time : 60 minutes
Servings : 4
Difficulty Level : Difficult

Ingredients:

- Olive oil cooking spray
- 1 large (about 1 pound) eggplant, sliced into ¼-inch-thick rounds
- 1 teaspoon kosher salt, divided
- 1 tablespoon extra-virgin olive oil
- 3 garlic cloves, minced
- 1 (28-ounce) can no-salt-added crushed tomatoes
- ½ teaspoon honey
- ¼ teaspoon freshly ground black pepper
- 2 tablespoons fresh basil, chopped
- 1 (15-ounce) can no-salt-added or low-sodium chickpeas, drained and rinsed
- ¾ cup crumbled feta cheese
- 1 tablespoon fresh oregano, chopped

Directions:

Preheat the oven to 425°F. Grease and line two baking sheets with foil and lightly spray with olive oil cooking spray. Spread the eggplant in a single layer and sprinkle with ½ teaspoon of the salt. Bake for 20 minutes, turning once halfway, until lightly golden brown.

Meanwhile, heat the olive oil in a large saucepan over medium heat. Mix in the garlic and sauté for 30 seconds. Add the crushed tomatoes, honey, the remaining ½ teaspoon salt, and black pepper. Simmer about 20 minutes, until the sauce reduces a bit and thickens. Stir in the basil.

After removing the eggplant from the oven, reduce the oven temperature to 375°F. In a large rectangular or oval baking dish, spoon in the chickpeas and 1 cup sauce. Layer the eggplant slices on top, overlapping as necessary to cover the chickpeas. Lay the remaining sauce on top of the eggplant. Sprinkle the feta cheese and oregano on top.

Wrap the baking dish with foil and bake for 15 minutes. Pull out the foil and bake an additional 15 minutes.

Nutrition (for 100g): 320 Calories 11g Fat 12g Carbohydrates 14g Protein 773mg Sodium

Baked Falafel Sliders

Preparation Time : 10 minutes

Cooking Time : 30 minutes

Servings : 6

Difficulty Level : Average

Ingredients:

- Olive oil cooking spray
- 1 (15-ounce) can low-sodium chickpeas, drained and rinsed
- 1 onion, roughly chopped
- 2 garlic cloves, peeled
- 2 tablespoons fresh parsley, chopped
- 2 tablespoons whole-wheat flour
- ½ teaspoon ground coriander
- ½ teaspoon ground cumin
- ½ teaspoon baking powder
- ½ teaspoon kosher salt
- ¼ teaspoon freshly ground black pepper

Directions:

Preheat the oven to 350°F. Put parchment paper or foil and lightly spray with olive oil cooking spray in the baking sheet.

In a food processor, mix in the chickpeas, onion, garlic, parsley, flour, coriander, cumin, baking powder, salt, and black pepper. Blend until smooth.

Make 6 slider patties, each with a heaping ¼ cup of mixture, and arrange on the prepared baking sheet. Bake for 30 minutes. Serve.

Nutrition (for 100g): 90 Calories 1g Fat 3g Carbohydrates 4g Protein 803mg Sodium

Portobello Caprese

Preparation Time : 15 minutes

Cooking Time : 30 minutes

Servings : 2

Difficulty Level : Difficult

Ingredients:

- 1 tablespoon olive oil
- 1 cup cherry tomatoes
- Salt and black pepper, to taste
- 4 large fresh basil leaves, thinly sliced, divided
- 3 medium garlic cloves, minced
- 2 large portobello mushrooms, stems removed
- 4 pieces mini Mozzarella balls
- 1 tablespoon Parmesan cheese, grated

Directions:

Prepare the oven to 350°F (180ºC). Grease a baking pan with olive oil. Drizzle 1 tablespoon olive oil in a nonstick skillet, and heat over medium-high heat. Add the tomatoes to the skillet, and sprinkle salt and black pepper to season. Prick some holes on the tomatoes for juice during the cooking. Put the lid on and cook the tomatoes for 10 minutes or until tender.

Reserve 2 teaspoons of basil and add the remaining basil and garlic to the skillet. Crush the tomatoes with a spatula, then cook for half a minute. Stir constantly during the cooking. Set aside. Arrange the mushrooms in the baking pan, cap side down, and sprinkle with salt and black pepper to taste.

Spoon the tomato mixture and Mozzarella balls on the gill of the mushrooms, then scatter with Parmesan cheese to coat well. Bake until the mushrooms are fork-tender and the cheeses are browned. Pull out the stuffed mushrooms from the oven and serve with basil on top.

Nutrition (for 100g): 285 Calories 21.8g Fat 2.1g Carbohydrates 14.3g Protein 823mg Sodium

Mushroom and Cheese Stuffed Tomatoes

Preparation Time : 15 minutes

Cooking Time : 20 minutes

Servings : 4

Difficulty Level : Average

Ingredients:

- 4 large ripe tomatoes
- 1 tablespoon olive oil
- ½ pound (454 g) white or cremini mushrooms, sliced
- 1 tablespoon fresh basil, chopped
- ½ cup yellow onion, diced
- 1 tablespoon fresh oregano, chopped
- 2 garlic cloves, minced
- ½ teaspoon salt
- ¼ teaspoon freshly ground black pepper
- 1 cup part-skim Mozzarella cheese, shredded
- 1 tablespoon Parmesan cheese, grated

Directions:

Ready the oven to 375°F (190ºC). Cut a ½-inch slice off the top of each tomato. Scoop the pulp into a bowl and leave ½-inch tomato shells. Arrange the tomatoes on a baking sheet lined with aluminum foil. Heat the olive oil in a nonstick skillet over medium heat.

Add the mushrooms, basil, onion, oregano, garlic, salt, and black pepper to the skillet and sauté for 5 minutes.

Pour the mixture to the tomato pulp bowl, then add the Mozzarella cheese and stir to combine well. Spoon the mixture into each tomato shell, then top with a layer of Parmesan. Bake in the preheated oven for 15 minutes or until the cheese is bubbly and the tomatoes are soft. Pull out the stuffed tomatoes from the oven and serve warm.

Nutrition (for 100g): 254 Calories 14.7g Fat 5.2g Carbohydrates 17.5g Protein 783mg Sodium

Tabbouleh

Preparation Time : 15 minutes
Cooking Time : 5 minutes
Servings : 6
Difficulty Level : Average

Ingredients:

- 4 tablespoons olive oil, divided
- 4 cups riced cauliflower
- 3 garlic cloves, finely minced
- Salt and black pepper, to taste
- ½ large cucumber, peeled, seeded, and chopped
- ½ cup Italian parsley, chopped
- Juice of 1 lemon
- 2 tablespoons minced red onion
- ½ cup mint leaves, chopped
- ½ cup pitted Kalamata olives, chopped
- 1 cup cherry tomatoes, quartered
- 2 cups baby arugula or spinach leaves
- 2 medium avocados, peeled, pitted, and diced

Directions:

Warm 2 tablespoons olive oil in a nonstick skillet over medium-high heat. Add the rice cauliflower, garlic, salt, and black pepper to the skillet and sauté for 3 minutes or until fragrant. Transfer them to a large bowl.

Add the cucumber, parsley, lemon juice, red onion, mint, olives, and remaining olive oil to the bowl. Toss to combine well. Reserve the bowl in the refrigerator for at least 30 minutes.

Remove the bowl from the refrigerator. Add the cherry tomatoes, arugula, avocado to the bowl. Season well, and toss to combine well. Serve chilled.

Nutrition (for 100g): 198 Calories 17.5g Fat 6.2g Carbohydrates 4.2g Protein 773mg Sodium

Spicy Broccoli Rabe And Artichoke Hearts

Preparation Time : 5 minutes

Cooking Time : 15 minutes

Servings : 4

Difficulty Level : Average

Ingredients:

- 3 tablespoons olive oil, divided
- 2 pounds (907 g) fresh broccoli rabe
- 3 garlic cloves, finely minced
- 1 teaspoon red pepper flakes
- 1 teaspoon salt, plus more to taste
- 13.5 ounces (383 g) artichoke hearts
- 1 tablespoon water
- 2 tablespoons red wine vinegar
- Freshly ground black pepper, to taste

Directions:

Warm 2 tablespoons olive oil in a nonstick skillet over medium-high skillet. Add the broccoli, garlic, red pepper flakes, and salt to the skillet and sauté for 5 minutes or until the broccoli is soft.

Put the artichoke hearts to the skillet and sauté for 2 more minutes or until tender. Add water to the skillet and turn down the heat to low. Put the lid on and simmer for 5 minutes. Meanwhile, combine the vinegar and 1 tablespoon of olive oil in a bowl.

Drizzle the simmered broccoli and artichokes with oiled vinegar, and sprinkle with salt and black pepper. Toss to combine well before serving.

Nutrition (for 100g): 272 Calories 21.5g Fat 9.8g Carbohydrates 11.2g Protein 736mg Sodium

Shakshuka

Preparation Time: 10 minutes

Cooking Time: 25 minutes

Servings: 4

Difficulty Level: Difficult

Ingredients:

- 5 tablespoons olive oil, divided
- 1 red bell pepper, finely diced
- ½ small yellow onion, finely diced
- 14 ounces (397 g) crushed tomatoes, with juices
- 6 ounces (170 g) frozen spinach, thawed and drained of excess liquid
- 1 teaspoon smoked paprika
- 2 garlic cloves, finely minced
- 2 teaspoons red pepper flakes
- 1 tablespoon capers, roughly chopped
- 1 tablespoon water
- 6 large eggs
- ¼ teaspoon freshly ground black pepper
- ¾ cup feta or goat cheese, crumbled
- ¼ cup fresh flat-leaf parsley or cilantro, chopped

Directions:

Ready the oven to 300ºF (150ºC). Heat 2 tablespoons olive oil in an oven-safe skillet over medium-high heat. Sauté the bell pepper and onion to the skillet until the onion is translucent and the bell pepper is soft.

Add the tomatoes and juices, spinach, paprika, garlic, red pepper flakes, capers, water, and 2 tablespoons olive oil to the skillet. Stir well and bring to a boil. Set down the heat to low, then put the lid on and simmer for 5 minutes.

Crack the eggs over the sauce, keep a little space between each egg, leave the egg intact and sprinkle with freshly ground black pepper. Cook until the eggs reach the right doneness.

Scatter the cheese over the eggs and sauce, and bake in the preheated oven for 5 minutes or until the cheese is frothy and golden brown. Drizzle with the remaining 1 tablespoon olive oil and spread the parsley on top before serving warm.

Nutrition (for 100g): 335 Calories 26.5g Fat 5g Carbohydrates 16.8g Protein 736mg Sodium

Spanakopita

Preparation Time : 15 minutes

Cooking Time : 50 minutes

Servings : 6

Difficulty Level : Difficult

Ingredients:

- 6 tablespoons olive oil, divided
- 1 small yellow onion, diced
- 4 cups frozen chopped spinach
- 4 garlic cloves, minced
- ½ teaspoon salt
- ½ teaspoon freshly ground black pepper
- 4 large eggs, beaten
- 1 cup ricotta cheese
- ¾ cup feta cheese, crumbled
- ¼ cup pine nuts

Directions:

Grease baking dish with 2 tablespoons olive oil. Organize the oven at 375 degrees F. Heat 2 tablespoons olive oil in a nonstick skillet over medium-high heat. Mix in the onion to the skillet and sauté for 6 minutes or until translucent and tender.

Add the spinach, garlic, salt, and black pepper to the skillet and sauté for 5 minutes more. Place them to a bowl and set aside.

Combine the beaten eggs and ricotta cheese in a separate bowl, then pour them in to the bowl of spinach mixture. Stir to mix well.

Fill the mixture into the baking dish, and tilt the dish so the mixture coats the bottom evenly. Bake until it begins to set. Take out the baking dish from the oven, and spread the feta cheese and pine nuts on top, then dash with remaining 2 tablespoons olive oil.

Return the baking dish to the oven and bake for another 15 minutes or until the top is golden brown. Remove the dish from the oven. Allow the spanakopita to cool for a few minutes and slice to serve.

Nutrition (for 100g): 340 Calories 27.3g Fat 10.1g Carbohydrates 18.2g Protein 781mg Sodium

Tagine

Preparation Time : 20 minutes
Cooking Time : 60 minutes
Servings : 6
Difficulty Level : Average

Ingredients:

- ½ cup olive oil
- 6 celery stalks, sliced into ¼-inch crescents
- 2 medium yellow onions, sliced
- 1 teaspoon ground cumin
- ½ teaspoon ground cinnamon
- 1 teaspoon ginger powder
- 6 garlic cloves, minced
- ½ teaspoon paprika
- 1 teaspoon salt
- ¼ teaspoon freshly ground black pepper
- 2 cups low-sodium vegetable stock
- 2 medium zucchinis, cut into ½-inch-thick semicircles
- 2 cups cauliflower, cut into florets
- 1 medium eggplant, cut into 1-inch cubes
- 1 cup green olives, halved and pitted
- 13.5 ounces (383 g) artichoke hearts, drained and quartered
- ½ cup chopped fresh cilantro leaves, for garnish
- ½ cup plain Greek yogurt, for garnish

- ½ cup chopped fresh flat-leaf parsley, for garnish

Directions:

Cook the olive oil in a stockpot over medium-high heat. Add the celery and onion to the pot and sauté for 6 minutes. Put the cumin, cinnamon, ginger, garlic, paprika, salt, and black pepper to the pot and sauté for 2 minutes more until aromatic.

Pour the vegetable stock to the pot and bring to a boil. Turn down the heat to low, and add the zucchini, cauliflower, and eggplant to the bank. Cover and simmer for 30 minutes or until the vegetables are soft. Then add the olives and artichoke hearts to the pool and simmer for 15 minutes more. Fill them into a large serving bowl or a Tagine, then serve with cilantro, Greek yogurt, and parsley on top.

Nutrition (for 100g): 312 Calories 21.2g Fat 9.2g Carbohydrates 6.1g Protein 813mg Sodium

Citrus Pistachios and Asparagus

Preparation Time : 10 minutes

Cooking Time : 10 minutes

Servings : 4

Difficulty Level : Difficult

Ingredients:

- Zest and juice of 2 clementine or 1 orange
- Zest and juice of 1 lemon
- 1 tablespoon red wine vinegar
- 3 tablespoons extra-virgin olive oil, divided
- 1 teaspoon salt, divided
- ¼ teaspoon freshly ground black pepper
- ½ cup pistachios, shelled
- 1 pound (454 g) fresh asparagus, trimmed
- 1 tablespoon water

Directions:

Combine the zest and juice of clementine and lemon, vinegar, 2 tablespoons of olive oil, ½ teaspoon of salt, and black pepper. Stir to mix well. Set aside.

Toast the pistachios in a nonstick skillet over medium-high heat for 2 minutes or until golden brown. Transfer the roasted pistachios to a clean work surface, then chop roughly. Mix the pistachios with the citrus mixture. Set aside.

Heat the remaining olive oil in the nonstick skillet over medium-high heat. Add the asparagus to the skillet and sauté for 2 minutes, then season with remaining salt. Add the water to the skillet. Put down the heat to low, and put the lid on. Simmer for 4 minutes until the asparagus is tender.

Remove the asparagus from the skillet to a large dish. Pour the citrus and pistachios mixture over the asparagus. Toss to coat well before serving.

Nutrition (for 100g): 211 Calories 17.5g Fat 3.8g Carbohydrates 5.9g Protein 901mg Sodium

Tomato and Parsley Stuffed Eggplant

Preparation Time : 15 minutes

Cooking Time : 2 hours and 10 minutes

Servings : 6

Difficulty Level : Average

Ingredients:

- ¼ cup extra-virgin olive oil
- 3 small eggplants, cut in half lengthwise
- 1 teaspoon sea salt
- ½ teaspoon freshly ground black pepper
- 1 large yellow onion, finely chopped
- 4 garlic cloves, minced
- 15 ounces (425 g) diced tomatoes, with the juice
- ¼ cup fresh flat-leaf parsley, finely chopped

Directions:

Put the insert of the slow cooker with 2 tablespoons of olive oil. Cut some slits on the cut side of each eggplant half, keep a ¼-inch space between each slit. Place the eggplant halves in the slow cooker, skin side down. Sprinkle with salt and black pepper.

Warm up the remaining olive oil in a nonstick skillet over medium-high heat. Add the onion and garlic to the skillet and sauté for 3 minutes or until the onion is translucent.

Add the parsley and tomatoes with the juice to the skillet, and sprinkle with salt and black pepper. Sauté for 5 more minutes or until they are tender. Divide and spoon the mixture in the skillet on the eggplant halves.

Situate the slow cooker lid on and cook on HIGH for 2 hours until the eggplant is soft. Transfer the eggplant to a plate, and allow to cool for a few minutes before serving.

Nutrition (for 100g): 455 Calories 13g Fat 14g Carbohydrates 14g Protein 719mg Sodium

Ratatouille

Preparation Time : 15 minutes

Cooking Time : 7 hours

Servings : 6

Difficulty Level : Average

Ingredients:

- 3 tablespoons extra-virgin olive oil
- 1 large eggplant, unpeeled, sliced
- 2 large onions, sliced
- 4 small zucchinis, sliced
- 2 green bell peppers
- 6 large tomatoes, cut in ½-inch wedges
- 2 tablespoons fresh flat-leaf parsley, chopped
- 1 teaspoon dried basil
- 2 garlic cloves, minced
- 2 teaspoons sea salt
- ¼ teaspoon freshly ground black pepper

Direction:

Fill the insert of the slow cooker with 2 tablespoons olive oil. Arrange the vegetables slices, strips, and wedges alternately in the insert of the slow cooker. Spread the parsley on top of the vegetables, and season with basil, garlic, salt, and black pepper. Drizzle with the remaining olive oil. Close and cook on LOW for 7 hours until the vegetables are tender. Transfer the vegetables on a plate and serve warm.

Nutrition (for 100g): 265 Calories 1.7g Fat 13.7g Carbohydrates 8.3g Protein 800mg Sodium

Gemista

Preparation Time : 15 minutes

Cooking Time : 4 hours

Servings : 4

Difficulty Level : Average

Ingredients:

- 2 tablespoons extra-virgin olive oil
- 4 large bell peppers, any color
- ½ cup uncooked couscous
- 1 teaspoon oregano
- 1 garlic clove, minced
- 1 cup crumbled feta cheese
- 1 (15-ounce / 425-g) can cannellini beans, rinsed and drained
- Salt and pepper, to taste
- 1 lemon wedges
- 4 green onions, white and green parts separated, thinly sliced

Direction:

Cut a ½-inch slice below the stem from the top of the bell pepper. Discard the stem only and chop the sliced top portion under the stem, and reserve in a bowl. Hollow the bell pepper with a spoon. Grease the slow cooker with oil.

Incorporate the remaining ingredients, except for the green parts of the green onion and lemon wedges, to the bowl of chopped bell pepper top. Stir to mix well. Spoon the mixture in the hollowed bell pepper, and arrange the stuffed bell peppers in the slow cooker, then drizzle with more olive oil.

Seal the slow cooker lid on and cook on HIGH for 4 hours or until the bell peppers are soft.

Remove the bell peppers from the slow cooker and serve on a plate. Sprinkle with green parts of the green onions, and squeeze the lemon wedges on top before serving.

Nutrition (for 100g): 246 Calories 9g Fat 6.5g Carbohydrates 11.1g Protein 698mg Sodium

Stuffed Cabbage Rolls

Preparation Time : 15 minutes

Cooking Time : 2 hours

Servings : 4

Difficulty Level : Difficult

Ingredients:

- 4 tablespoons olive oil, divided
- 1 large head green cabbage, cored
- 1 large yellow onion, chopped
- 3 ounces (85 g) feta cheese, crumbled
- ½ cup dried currants
- 3 cups cooked pearl barley
- 2 tablespoons fresh flat-leaf parsley, chopped
- 2 tablespoons pine nuts, toasted
- ½ teaspoon sea salt
- ½ teaspoon black pepper
- 15 ounces (425 g) crushed tomatoes, with the juice
- 1 tablespoon apple cider vinegar
- ½ cup apple juice

Directions:

Brush off the insert of the slow cooker with 2 tablespoons olive oil. Blanch the cabbage in a pot of water for 8 minutes. Take it from the water, and set aside, then separate 16 leaves from the cabbage. Set aside.

Drizzle the remaining olive oil in a nonstick skillet, and heat over medium heat. Stir in the onion to the skillet and cook until the onion and bell pepper is tender. Transfer the onion to a bowl.

Add the feta cheese, currants, barley, parsley, and pine nuts to the bowl of cooked onion, then sprinkle with ¼ teaspoon of salt and ¼ teaspoon of black pepper.

Arrange the cabbage leaves on a clean work surface. Scoop 1/3 cup of the mixture on the center of each plate, then fold the edge onto the mixture and roll it up. Place the cabbage rolls in the slow cooker, seam side down.

Incorporate the remaining ingredients in a separate bowl, then pour the mixture over the cabbage rolls. Seal slow cooker lid on and cook on HIGH for 2 hours. Remove the cabbage rolls from the slow cooker and serve warm.

Nutrition (for 100g): 383 Calories 14.7g Fat 12.9g Carbohydrates 10.7g Protein 838mg Sodium

Brussels Sprouts with Balsamic Glaze

Preparation Time : 15 minutes
Cooking Time : 2 hours
Servings : 6
Difficulty Level : Average

Ingredients:

- Balsamic Glaze:
- 1 cup balsamic vinegar
- ¼ cup honey
- 2 tablespoons extra-virgin olive oil
- 2 pounds (907 g) Brussels sprouts, trimmed and halved
- 2 cups low-sodium vegetable soup
- 1 teaspoon sea salt
- Freshly ground black pepper, to taste
- ¼ cup Parmesan cheese, grated
- ¼ cup pine nuts

Directions:

Make the balsamic glaze: Combine the balsamic vinegar and honey in a saucepan. Stir to mix well. Over medium-high heat, bring to a boil. Set down the heat to low, then simmer for 20 minutes or until the glaze reduces in half and has a thick consistency. Impose some olive oil inside the insert of the slow cooker.

Put the Brussels sprouts, vegetable soup, and ½ teaspoon of salt in the slow cooker, stir to combine. Seal the slow cooker lid on and cook on HIGH for 2 hours until the Brussels sprouts are soft.

Put the Brussels sprouts to a plate, and sprinkle the remaining salt and black pepper to season. Dash the balsamic glaze over the Brussels sprouts, then serve with Parmesan and pine nuts.

Nutrition (for 100g): 270 Calories 10.6g Fat 6.9g Carbohydrates 8.7g Protein 693mg Sodium

Spinach Salad with Citrus Vinaigrette

Preparation Time : 10 minutes
Cooking Time : 0 minutes
Servings : 4
Difficulty Level : Easy

Ingredients:

- Citrus Vinaigrette:
- ¼ cup extra-virgin olive oil
- 3 tablespoons balsamic vinegar
- ½ teaspoon fresh lemon zest
- ½ teaspoon salt
- Salad:
- 1-pound (454 g) baby spinach, washed, stems removed
- 1 large ripe tomato, cut into ¼-inch pieces
- 1 medium red onion, thinly sliced

Directions:

Make the citrus vinaigrette: Stir together the olive oil, balsamic vinegar, lemon zest, and salt in a bowl until mixed well.

Make the salad: Place the baby spinach, tomato and onions in a separate salad bowl. Fill the citrus vinaigrette over the salad and gently toss until the vegetables are coated thoroughly.

Nutrition (for 100g): 173 Calories 14.2g Fat 4.2g Carbohydrates 4.1g Protein 699mg Sodium

Simple Celery and Orange Salad

Preparation Time : 15 minutes

Cooking Time : 0 minutes

Servings : 6

Difficulty Level : Easy

Ingredients:

- Salad:
- 3 celery stalks, including leaves, sliced diagonally into ½-inch slices
- ½ cup green olives
- ¼ cup sliced red onion
- 2 large peeled oranges, cut into rounds
- Dressing:
- 1 tablespoon extra-virgin olive oil
- 1 tablespoon lemon or orange juice
- 1 tablespoon olive brine
- ¼ teaspoon kosher or sea salt
- ¼ teaspoon freshly ground black pepper

Directions:

Make the salad: Put the celery stalks, green olives, onion, and oranges in a shallow bowl. Mix well and set aside.

Make the dressing: Stir the olive oil, lemon juice, olive brine, salt, and pepper well.

Fill the dressing into the bowl of salad and lightly toss until coated thoroughly.

Serve chilled or at room temperature.

Nutrition (for 100g): 24 Calories 1.2g Fat 1.2g Carbohydrates 1.1g Protein 813mg Sodium

Fried Eggplant Rolls

Preparation Time : 20 minutes

Cooking Time : 10 minutes

Servings : 6

Difficulty Level : Average

Ingredients:

- 2 large eggplants
- 1 teaspoon salt
- 1 cup shredded ricotta cheese
- 4 ounces (113 g) goat cheese, shredded
- ¼ cup finely chopped fresh basil
- ½ teaspoon freshly ground black pepper
- Olive oil spray

Directions:

Add the eggplant slices to a colander and season with salt. Set aside for 15 to 20 minutes.

Mix together the ricotta and goat cheese, basil, and black pepper in a large bowl and stir to combine. Set aside. Pat dry the eggplant slices with paper towels and lightly mist them with olive oil spray.

Warm up large skillet over medium heat and lightly spray it with olive oil spray. Arrange the eggplant slices in the skillet and fry each side for 3 minutes until golden brown.

Remove from the heat to a paper towel-lined plate and rest for 5 minutes. Make the eggplant rolls: Lay the eggplant slices on a flat work surface and top each slice with a tablespoon of the prepared cheese mixture. Roll them up and serve immediately.

Nutrition (for 100g): 254 Calories 14.9g Fat 7.1g Carbohydrates 15.3g Protein 612mg Sodium

Roasted Veggies and Brown Rice Bowl

Preparation Time : 15 minutes

Cooking Time : 20 minutes

Servings : 4

Difficulty Level : Average

Ingredients:

- 2 cups cauliflower florets
- 2 cups broccoli florets
- 1 (15-ounce / 425-g) can chickpeas
- 1 cup carrot slices (about 1 inch thick)
- 2 to 3 tablespoons extra-virgin olive oil, divided
- Salt and black pepper, to taste
- Nonstick cooking spray
- 2 cups cooked brown rice
- 3 tablespoons sesame seeds
- <u>Dressing:</u>
- 3 to 4 tablespoons tahini
- 2 tablespoons honey
- 1 lemon, juiced
- 1 garlic clove, minced
- Salt and black pepper, to taste

Directions:

Ready the oven to 400ºF (205ºC). Spritz two baking sheets with nonstick cooking spray.

Spread the cauliflower and broccoli on the first baking sheet and the second with the chickpeas and carrot slices.

Drizzle each sheet with half of the olive oil and sprinkle with salt and pepper. Toss to coat well.

Roast the chickpeas and carrot slices in the preheated oven for 10 minutes, leaving the carrots tender but crisp, and the cauliflower and broccoli for 20 minutes until fork-tender. Stir them once halfway through the cooking time.

Meanwhile, make the dressing: Whisk together the tahini, honey, lemon juice, garlic, salt, and pepper in a small bowl.

Divide the cooked brown rice among four bowls. Top each bowl evenly with roasted vegetables and dressing. Sprinkle the sesame seeds on top for garnish before serving.

Nutrition (for 100g): 453 Calories 17.8g Fat 11.2g Carbohydrates 12.1g Protein 793mg Sodium

Cauliflower Hash with Carrots

Preparation Time : 10 minutes

Cooking Time : 10 minutes

Servings : 4

Difficulty Level : Easy

Ingredients:

- 3 tablespoons extra-virgin olive oil
- 1 large onion, chopped
- 1 tablespoon minced garlic
- 2 cups diced carrots
- 4 cups cauliflower florets
- ½ teaspoon ground cumin
- 1 teaspoon salt

Directions:

Cook the olive oil over medium heat. Mix in the onion and garlic and sauté for 1 minute. Stir in the carrots and stir-fry for 3 minutes. Add the cauliflower florets, cumin, and salt and toss to combine.

Cover and cook for 3 minutes until lightly browned. Stir well and cook, uncovered, for 3 to 4 minutes, until softened. Remove from the heat and serve warm.

Nutrition (for 100g): 158 Calories 10.8g Fat 5.1g Carbohydrates 3.1g Protein 813mg Sodium

Garlicky Zucchini Cubes with Mint

Preparation Time : 5 minutes

Cooking Time : 10 minutes

Servings : 4

Difficulty Level : Easy

Ingredients:

- 3 large green zucchinis
- 3 tablespoons extra-virgin olive oil
- 1 large onion, chopped
- 3 cloves garlic, minced
- 1 teaspoon salt
- 1 teaspoon dried mint

Directions:

Cook the olive oil in a large skillet over medium heat.

Mix in the onion and garlic and sauté for 3 minutes, stirring constantly, or until softened.

Stir in the zucchini cubes and salt and cook for 5 minutes, or until the zucchini is browned and tender.

Add the mint to the skillet and toss to combine, then continue cooking for 2 minutes. Serve warm.

Nutrition (for 100g): 146 Calories 10.6g Fat 3g Carbohydrates 4.2g Protein 789mg Sodium

Zucchini and Artichokes Bowl with Faro

Preparation Time : 15 minutes

Cooking Time : 10 minutes

Servings : 6

Difficulty Level : Easy

Ingredients:

- 1/3 cup extra-virgin olive oil
- 1/3 cup chopped red onions
- ½ cup chopped red bell pepper
- 2 garlic cloves, minced
- 1 cup zucchini, cut into ½-inch-thick slices
- ½ cup coarsely chopped artichokes
- ½ cup canned chickpeas, drained and rinsed
- 3 cups cooked faro
- Salt and black pepper, to taste
- ½ cup crumbled feta cheese, for serving (optional)
- ¼ cup sliced olives, for serving (optional)
- 2 tablespoons fresh basil, chiffonade, for serving (optional)
- 3 tablespoons balsamic vinegar, for serving (optional)

Directions:

Heat up the olive oil in a large skillet over medium heat until it shimmers. Mix the onions, bell pepper, and garlic and sauté for 5 minutes, stirring occasionally, until softened.

Stir in the zucchini slices, artichokes, and chickpeas and sauté for about 5 minutes until slightly tender. Add the cooked faro and toss to combine until heated through. Sprinkle the salt and pepper to season.

Divide the mixture into bowls. Top each bowl evenly with feta cheese, olive slices, and basil and sprinkle with the balsamic vinegar, if desired.

Nutrition (for 100g): 366 Calories 19.9g Fat 9g Carbohydrates 9.3g Protein 819mg Sodium

5-Ingredient Zucchini Fritters

Preparation Time : 15 minutes

Cooking Time : 5 minutes

Servings : 14

Difficulty Level : Average

Ingredients:

- 4 cups grated zucchini
- Salt, to taste
- 2 large eggs, slightly beaten
- 1/3 cup sliced scallions
- 2/3 all-purpose flour
- 1/8 teaspoon black pepper
- 2 tablespoons olive oil

Directions:

Situate the grated zucchini in a colander and lightly season with salt. Set aside to rest for 10 minutes. Grip as much liquid from the grated zucchini as possible.

Pour the grated zucchini into a bowl. Fold in the beaten eggs, scallions, flour, salt, and pepper and stir until everything is well combined.

Heat up the olive oil in a large skillet over medium heat until hot.

Drop 3 tablespoons mounds of the zucchini mixture onto the hot skillet to make each fritter, pin them lightly into rounds and spacing them about 2 inches apart.

Cook for 2 to 3 minutes. Flip the zucchini fritters and cook for 2 minutes more, or until they are golden brown and cooked through.

Remove from the heat to a plate lined with paper towels. Repeat with the remaining zucchini mixture. Serve hot.

Nutrition (for 100g): 113 Calories 6.1g Fat 9g Carbohydrates 4g Protein 793mg Sodium

Garlic-Roasted Tomatoes and Olives

Preparation Time : 5 minutes

Cooking Time : 20 minutes

Servings : 6

Difficulty Level : Easy

Ingredients:

- 2 cups cherry tomatoes
- 4 garlic cloves, roughly chopped
- ½ red onion, roughly chopped
- 1 cup black olives
- 1 cup green olives
- 1 tablespoon fresh basil, minced
- 1 tablespoon fresh oregano, minced
- 2 tablespoons olive oil
- ¼ to ½ teaspoon salt

Directions:

Preheat the air fryer to 380°F. In a large bowl, incorporate all of the ingredients and toss together so that the tomatoes and olives are coated well with the olive oil and herbs.

Pour the mixture into the air fryer basket, and roast for 10 minutes. Stir the mixture well, then continue roasting for an additional 10 minutes. Remove from the air fryer, transfer to a serving bowl, and enjoy.

Nutrition (for 100g): 109 Calories 10g Fat 5g Carbohydrates 1g Protein 647mg Sodium

Goat Cheese and Garlic Crostini

Preparation Time : 3 minutes
Cooking Time : 5 minutes
Servings : 4
Difficulty Level : Average

Ingredients:

- 1 whole wheat baguette
- ¼ cup olive oil
- 2 garlic cloves, minced
- 4 ounces goat cheese
- 2 tablespoons fresh basil, minced

Directions:

Preheat the air fryer to 380°F. Cut the baguette into ½-inch-thick slices. In a small bowl, incorporate together the olive oil and garlic, then brush it over one side of each slice of bread.

Place the olive-oil-coated bread in a single layer in the air fryer basket and bake for 5 minutes. In the meantime, combine together the goat cheese and basil. Remove the toast from the air fryer, then spread a thin layer of the goat cheese mixture over on each piece and serve.

Nutrition (for 100g): 365 Calories 21g Fat 10g Carbohydrates 12g Protein 804mg Sodium

Rosemary-Roasted Red Potatoes

Preparation Time : 5 minutes

Cooking Time : 20 minutes

Servings : 6

Difficulty Level : Easy

Ingredients:

- 1-pound red potatoes, quartered
- ¼ cup olive oil
- ½ teaspoon kosher salt
- ¼ teaspoon black pepper
- 1 garlic clove, minced
- 4 rosemary sprigs

Directions:

Preheat the air fryer to 360°F.

In a large bowl, toss in the potatoes with the olive oil, salt, pepper, and garlic until well coated. Fill the air fryer basket with potatoes and top with the sprigs of rosemary.

Roast for 10 minutes, then stir or toss the potatoes and roast for 10 minutes more. Remove the rosemary sprigs and serve the potatoes. Season well.

Nutrition (for 100g): 133 Calories 9g Fat 5g Carbohydrates 1g Protein 617mg Sodium

Avocado Egg Scramble

Preparation Time : 8 minutes

Cooking Time : 15 minutes

Servings : 4

Difficulty Level : Average

Ingredients:

- 4 eggs, beaten
- 1 white onion, diced
- 1 tablespoon avocado oil
- 1 avocado, finely chopped
- ½ teaspoon chili flakes
- 1 oz Cheddar cheese, shredded
- ½ teaspoon salt
- 1 tablespoon fresh parsley

Directions:

Pour avocado oil in the skillet and bring it to boil. Then add diced onion and roast it until it is light brown. Meanwhile, mix up together chili flakes, beaten eggs, and salt.

Fill the egg mixture over the cooked onion and cook the mixture for 1 minute over the medium heat. After this, scramble the eggs well with the help of the fork or spatula. Cook the eggs until they are solid but soft.

After this, add chopped avocado and shredded cheese. Stir the scramble well and transfer in the serving plates. Sprinkle the meal with fresh parsley.

Nutrition (for 100g): 236 Calories 20g Fat 4g Carbohydrates 8.6g Protein 804mg Sodium

Morning Tostadas

Preparation Time : 15 minutes

Cooking Time : 6 minutes

Servings : 6

Difficulty Level : Difficult

Ingredients :

- ½ white onion, diced
- 1 tomato, chopped
- 1 cucumber, chopped
- 1 tablespoon fresh cilantro, chopped
- ½ jalapeno pepper, chopped
- 1 tablespoon lime juice
- 6 corn tortillas
- 1 tablespoon canola oil
- 2 oz Cheddar cheese, shredded
- ½ cup white beans, canned, drained
- 6 eggs
- ½ teaspoon butter
- ½ teaspoon Sea salt

Directions:

Make Pico de Galo: in the salad bowl combine together diced white onion, tomato, cucumber, fresh cilantro, and jalapeno pepper. Then add lime juice and a ½ tablespoon of canola oil. Mix up the mixture well. Pico de Galo is cooked. After this, preheat the oven to

390F. Line the tray with baking paper. Arrange the corn tortillas on the baking paper and brush with remaining canola oil from both sides. Bake the tortillas until they start to be crunchy. Chill the cooked crunchy tortillas well. Meanwhile, toss the butter in the skillet.

Crack the eggs in the melted butter and sprinkle them with sea salt. Fry the eggs until the egg whites become white (cooked). Approximately for 3-5 minutes over the medium heat. After this, mash the beans until you get puree texture. Spread the bean puree on the corn tortillas. Add fried eggs. Then top the eggs with Pico de Galo and shredded Cheddar cheese.

Nutrition (for 100g): 246 Calories 11g Fat 4.7g Carbohydrates 13.7g Protein 593mg Sodium

Parmesan Omelet

Preparation Time : 5 minutes
Cooking Time : 10 minutes
Servings : 2
Difficulty Level : Easy

Ingredients:

- 1 tablespoon cream cheese
- 2 eggs, beaten
- ¼ teaspoon paprika
- ½ teaspoon dried oregano
- ¼ teaspoon dried dill
- 1 oz Parmesan, grated
- 1 teaspoon coconut oil

Directions:

Mix up together cream cheese with eggs, dried oregano, and dill. Pour coconut oil in the skillet and heat it up until it will coat all the skillet. Then fill the skillet with the egg mixture and flatten it. Add grated Parmesan and close the lid. Cook omelet for 10 minutes over the low heat. Then transfer the cooked omelet in the serving plate and sprinkle with paprika.

Nutrition (for 100g): 148 Calories 11.5g Fat 0.3g Carbohydrates 10.6g Protein 741mg Sodium

Watermelon Pizza

Preparation Time : 10 minutes

Cooking Time : 0 minutes

Servings : 2

Difficulty Level : Easy

Ingredients:

- 9 oz watermelon slice
- 1 tablespoon Pomegranate sauce
- 2 oz Feta cheese, crumbled
- 1 tablespoon fresh cilantro, chopped

Directions:

Place the watermelon slice in the plate and sprinkle with crumbled Feta cheese. Add fresh cilantro. After this, sprinkle the pizza with Pomegranate juice generously. Cut the pizza into the servings.

Nutrition (for 100g): 143 Calories 6.2g Fat 0.6g Carbohydrates 5.1g Protein 811mg Sodium

Savory Muffins

Preparation Time : 10 minutes

Cooking Time : 15 minutes

Servings : 4

Difficulty Level : Average

Ingredients:

- 3 oz ham, chopped
- 4 eggs, beaten
- 2 tablespoons coconut flour
- ½ teaspoon dried oregano
- ¼ teaspoon dried cilantro
- Cooking spray

Directions:

Spray the muffin's molds with cooking spray from inside. In the bowl mix up together beaten eggs, coconut flour, dried oregano, cilantro, and ham. When the liquid is homogenous, pour it in the prepared muffin molds.

Bake the muffins for 15 minutes at 360F. Chill the cooked meal well and only after this remove from the molds.

Nutrition (for 100g): 128 Calories 7.2g Fat 2.9g Carbohydrates 10.1g Protein 882mg Sodium

Morning Pizza with Sprouts

Preparation Time : 15 minutes

Cooking Time : 20 minutes

Servings : 6

Difficulty Level : Average

Ingredients :

- ½ cup wheat flour, whole grain
- 2 tablespoons butter, softened
- ¼ teaspoon baking powder
- ¾ teaspoon salt
- 5 oz chicken fillet, boiled
- 2 oz Cheddar cheese, shredded
- 1 teaspoon tomato sauce
- 1 oz bean sprouts

Directions :

Make the pizza crust: mix up together wheat flour, butter, baking powder, and salt. Knead the soft and non-sticky dough. Add more wheat flour if needed. Leave the dough for 10 minutes to chill. Then place the dough on the baking paper. Cover it with the second baking paper sheet.

Roll up the dough with the help of the rolling pin to get the round pizza crust. After this, remove the upper baking paper sheet. Transfer the pizza crust in the tray.

Spread the crust with tomato sauce. Then shred the chicken fillet and arrange it over the pizza crust. Add shredded Cheddar cheese. Bake pizza for 20 minutes at 355F. Then top the cooked pizza with bean sprouts and slice into the servings.

Nutrition (for 100g): 157 Calories 8.8g Fat 0.3g Carbohydrates 10.5g Protein 753mg Sodium

Banana Quinoa

Preparation Time : 10 minutes

Cooking Time : 12 minutes

Servings : 4

Difficulty Level : Easy

Ingredients:

- 1 cup quinoa
- 2 cup milk
- 1 teaspoon vanilla extract
- 1 teaspoon honey
- 2 bananas, sliced
- ¼ teaspoon ground cinnamon

Directions:

Pour milk in the saucepan and add quinoa. Close the lid and cook it over the medium heat for 12 minutes or until quinoa will absorb all liquid. Then chill the quinoa for 10-15 minutes and place in the serving mason jars.

Add honey, vanilla extract, and ground cinnamon. Stir well. Top quinoa with banana and stirs it before serving.

Nutrition (for 100g): 279 Calories 5.3g Fat 4.6g Carbohydrates 10.7g Protein 581mg Sodium

Egg Casserole with Paprika

Preparation Time : 10 minutes

Cooking Time : 28 minutes

Servings : 4

Difficulty Level : Average

Ingredients:

- 2 eggs, beaten
- 1 red bell pepper, chopped
- 1 chili pepper, chopped
- ½ red onion, diced
- 1 teaspoon canola oil
- ½ teaspoon salt
- 1 teaspoon paprika
- 1 tablespoon fresh cilantro, chopped
- 1 garlic clove, diced
- 1 teaspoon butter, softened
- ¼ teaspoon chili flakes

Directions:

Brush the casserole mold with canola oil and pour beaten eggs inside. After this, toss the butter in the skillet and melt it over the medium heat. Add chili pepper and red bell pepper.

After this, add red onion and cook the vegetables for 7-8 minutes over the medium heat. Stir them from time to time. Transfer the vegetables in the casserole mold.

Add salt, paprika, cilantro, diced garlic, and chili flakes. Stir mildly with the help of a spatula to get a homogenous mixture. Bake the casserole for 20 minutes at 355F in the oven. Then chill the meal well and cut into servings. Transfer the casserole in the serving plates with the help of the spatula.

Nutrition (for 100g): 68 Calories 4.5g Fat 1g Carbohydrates 3.4g Protein 882mg Sodium

Cauliflower Fritters

Preparation Time : 10 minutes

Cooking Time : 10 minutes

Servings : 2

Difficulty Level : Easy

Ingredients :

- 1 cup cauliflower, shredded
- 1 egg, beaten
- 1 tablespoon wheat flour, whole grain
- 1 oz Parmesan, grated
- ½ teaspoon ground black pepper
- 1 tablespoon canola oil

Directions:

In the mixing bowl mix up together shredded cauliflower and egg. Add wheat flour, grated Parmesan, and ground black pepper. Stir the mixture with the help of the fork until it is homogenous and smooth.

Pour canola oil in the skillet and bring it to boil. Make the fritters from the cauliflower mixture with the help of the fingertips or use spoon and transfer in the hot oil. Roast the fritters for 4 minutes from each side over the medium-low heat.

Nutrition (for 100g): 167 Calories 12.3g Fat 1.5g Carbohydrates 8.8g Protein 705mg Sodium

Creamy Oatmeal with Figs

Preparation Time : 10 minutes

Cooking Time : 20 minutes

Servings : 5

Difficulty Level : Easy

Ingredients:

- 2 cups oatmeal
- 1 ½ cup milk
- 1 tablespoon butter
- 3 figs, chopped
- 1 tablespoon honey

Directions:

Pour milk in the saucepan. Add oatmeal and close the lid. Cook the oatmeal for 15 minutes over the medium-low heat. Then add chopped figs and honey.

Add butter and mix up the oatmeal well. Cook it for 5 minutes more. Close the lid and let the cooked breakfast rest for 10 minutes before serving.

Nutrition (for 100g): 222 Calories 6g Fat 4.4g Carbohydrates 7.1g Protein 822mg Sodium

Baked Oatmeal with Cinnamon

Preparation Time : 10 minutes

Cooking Time : 25 minutes

Servings : 4

Difficulty Level : Easy

Ingredients:

- 1 cup oatmeal
- 1/3 cup milk
- 1 pear, chopped
- 1 teaspoon vanilla extract
- 1 tablespoon Splenda
- 1 teaspoon butter
- ½ teaspoon ground cinnamon
- 1 egg, beaten

Directions:

In the big bowl mix up together oatmeal, milk, egg, vanilla extract, Splenda, and ground cinnamon. Melt butter and add it in the oatmeal mixture. Then add chopped pear and stir it well.

Transfer the oatmeal mixture in the casserole mold and flatten gently. Cover it with the foil and secure edges. Bake the oatmeal for 25 minutes at 350F.

Nutrition (for 100g): 151 Calories 3.9g Fat 3.3g Carbohydrates 4.9g Protein 753mg Sodium

Almond Chia Porridge

Preparation Time : 10 minutes

Cooking Time : 30 minutes

Servings : 4

Difficulty Level : Easy

Ingredients:

- 3 cups organic almond milk
- 1/3 cup chia seeds, dried
- 1 teaspoon vanilla extract
- 1 tablespoon honey
- ¼ teaspoon ground cardamom

Directions:

Pour almond milk in the saucepan and bring it to boil. Then chill the almond milk to the room temperature (or appx. For 10-15 minutes). Add vanilla extract, honey, and ground cardamom. Stir well. After this, add chia seeds and stir again. Close the lid and let chia seeds soak the liquid for 20-25 minutes. Transfer the cooked porridge into the serving ramekins.

Nutrition (for 100g): 150 Calories 7.3g Fat 6.1g Carbohydrates 3.7g Protein 836mg Sodium

Cocoa Oatmeal

Preparation Time : 10 minutes
Cooking Time : 15 minutes
Servings : 2
Difficulty Level : Easy

Ingredients:

- 1 ½ cup oatmeal
- 1 tablespoon cocoa powder
- ½ cup heavy cream
- ¼ cup of water
- 1 teaspoon vanilla extract
- 1 tablespoon butter
- 2 tablespoons Splenda

Directions :

Mix up together oatmeal with cocoa powder and Splenda. Transfer the mixture in the saucepan. Add vanilla extract, water, and heavy cream. Stir it gently with the help of the spatula.

Close the lid and cook it for 10-15 minutes over the medium-low heat. Remove the cooked cocoa oatmeal from the heat and add butter. Stir it well.

Nutrition (for 100g): 230 Calories 10.6g Fat 3.5g Carbohydrates 4.6g Protein 691mg Sodium

Cinnamon Roll Oats

Preparation Time : 7 minutes

Cooking Time : 10 minutes

Servings : 4

Difficulty Level : Easy

Ingredients:

- ½ cup rolled oats
- 1 cup milk
- 1 teaspoon vanilla extract
- 1 teaspoon ground cinnamon
- 2 teaspoon honey
- 2 tablespoons Plain yogurt
- 1 teaspoon butter

Directions:

Transfer milk in the saucepan and bring it to boil. Add rolled oats and stir well. Close the lid and simmer the oats for 5 minutes over the medium heat. The cooked oats will absorb all milk.

Then add butter and stir the oats well. In the separated bowl, whisk together Plain yogurt with honey, cinnamon, and vanilla extract. Transfer the cooked oats in the serving bowls. Top the oats with the yogurt mixture in the shape of the wheel.

Nutrition (for 100g): 243 Calories 20.2g Fat 1g Carbohydrates 13.3g Protein 697mg Sodium

Pumpkin Oatmeal with Spices

Preparation Time : 10 minutes

Cooking Time : 13 minutes

Servings : 6

Difficulty Level : Easy

Ingredients :

- 2 cups oatmeal
- 1 cup of coconut milk
- 1 cup milk
- 1 teaspoon Pumpkin pie spices
- 2 tablespoons pumpkin puree
- 1 tablespoon Honey
- ½ teaspoon butter

Directions:

Pour coconut milk and milk in the saucepan. Add butter and bring the liquid to boil. Add oatmeal, stir well with the help of a spoon and close the lid.

Simmer the oatmeal for 7 minutes over the medium heat. Meanwhile, mix up together honey, pumpkin pie spices, and pumpkin puree. When the oatmeal is cooked, add pumpkin puree mixture and stir well. Transfer the cooked breakfast in the serving plates.

Nutrition (for 100g): 232 Calories 12.5g Fat 3.8g Carbohydrates 5.9g Protein 708mg Sodium

Stewed Cinnamon Apples with Dates

Preparation Time : 15 minutes

Cooking Time : 10 minutes

Servings : 6

Difficulty Level : Easy

Ingredients:

- 4 large Pink Lady apples
- ½ cup water
- ¼ cup chopped pitted dates
- 1 teaspoon ground cinnamon
- ¼ teaspoon vanilla extract
- 1 teaspoon unsalted butter

Directions:

Place apples, water, dates, and cinnamon in the Instant Pot®. Close, let steam release, press the Manual button, and set the timer to 3 minutes.

When the alarm beeps, quick-release the pressure until the float valve sets. Click the Cancel button and open lid. Stir in vanilla and butter. Serve hot or chilled.

Nutrition (for 100g): 111 Calories 2g Fat 6g Carbohydrates 1g Protein 411mg Sodium

Spiced Poached Pears

Preparation Time : 10 minutes

Cooking Time : 15 minutes

Servings : 4

Difficulty Level : Easy

Ingredients:

- 2 cups water
- 2 cups red wine
- ¼ cup honey
- 4 whole cloves
- 2 cinnamon sticks
- 1-star anise
- 1 teaspoon vanilla bean paste
- 4 Bartlett pears, peeled

Directions:

Place all elements in the Instant Pot® and mix. Cover, set steam release to Sealing, press the Manual Instant Pot®. Stir to couple. Close lid, let steam release to Seal click the Manual button, and alarm to 3 minutes.

When the timer beeps, swiftly-release the pressure until the float valve drops. Select the Cancel and open. Take out pears to a plate and allow to cool for 5 minutes. Serve warm.

Nutrition (for 100g): 194 Calories 5g Fat 4g Carbohydrates 1g Protein 366mg Sodium

Cranberry Applesauce

Preparation Time : 10 minutes

Cooking Time : 20 minutes

Servings : 8

Difficulty Level : Easy

Ingredients:

- 1 cup whole cranberries
- 4 medium tart apples, peeled, cored, and grated
- 4 medium sweet apples, peeled, cored, and grated
- 1½ tablespoons grated orange zest
- ¼ cup orange juice
- ¼ cup dark brown sugar
- ¼ cup granulated sugar
- 1 tablespoon unsalted butter
- 2 teaspoons ground cinnamon
- ½ teaspoon ground cloves
- ¼ teaspoon ground black pepper
- 1/8 teaspoon salt
- 1 tablespoon lemon juice

Directions:

Incorporate all ingredients in the Instant Pot®. Seal then, set the Manual button, and time to 5 minutes. When the timer beeps, let pressure release naturally, about 25 minutes. Open the lid. Lightly mash fruit with a fork. Stir well. Serve warm or cold.

Nutrition (for 100g): 136 Calories 4g Fat 3g Carbohydrates 9g Protein 299mg Sodium

Blueberry Compote

Preparation Time : 10 minutes

Cooking Time : 0 minutes

Servings : 8

Difficulty Level : Average

Ingredients:

- 1 (16-ounce) bag frozen blueberries, thawed
- ¼ cup sugar
- 1 tablespoon lemon juice
- 2 tablespoons cornstarch
- 2 tablespoons water
- ¼ teaspoon vanilla extract
- ¼ teaspoon grated lemon zest

Directions:

Add blueberries, sugar, and lemon juice to the Instant Pot®. Cover and press the Manual button, and adjust time to 1 minute.

When the timer beeps, sharply-release the pressure until the float valve falls. Press the Cancel button and open it.

Press the Sauté button. Combine cornstarch and water. Stir into blueberry mixture and cook until mixture comes to a boil and thickens, about 3–4 minutes. Press the Cancel button and stir in vanilla and lemon zest. Serve immediately or refrigerate until ready to serve.

Nutrition (for 100g): 57 Calories 2g Fat 14g Carbohydrates 7g Protein 348mg Sodium

Dried Fruit Compote

Preparation Time : 5 minutes

Cooking Time : 20 minutes

Servings : 6

Difficulty Level : Average

Ingredients:

- 8 ounces dried apricots, quartered
- 8 ounces dried peaches, quartered
- 1 cup golden raisins
- 1½ cups orange juice
- 1 cinnamon stick
- 4 whole cloves

Directions:

Stir to merge. Close, select the Manual button, and adjust the time to 3 minutes. When the timer beeps, let pressure release naturally, about 20 minutes. Press the Cancel button and open lid.

Remove and discard cinnamon stick and cloves. Press the Sauté button and simmer for 5-6 minutes. Serve warm then cover and refrigerate for up to a week.

Nutrition (for 100g): 258 Calories 5g Fat 8g Carbohydrates 4g Protein 277mg Sodium

Chocolate Rice Pudding

Preparation Time : 10 minutes

Cooking Time : 20 minutes

Servings : 6

Difficulty Level : Easy

Ingredients:

- 2 cups almond milk
- 1 cup long-grain brown rice
- 2 tablespoons Dutch-processed cocoa powder
- ¼ cup maple syrup
- 1 teaspoon vanilla extract
- ½ cup chopped dark chocolate

Directions:

Place almond milk, rice, cocoa, maple syrup, and vanilla in the Instant Pot®. Close then select the Manual button, and set time to 20 minutes. When the timer beeps, let pressure release naturally for 15 minutes, then quick-release the remaining pressure. Press the Cancel button and open lid. Serve warm, sprinkled with chocolate.

Nutrition (for 100g): 271 Calories 8g Fat 4g Carbohydrates 3g Protein 360mg Sodium

Fruit Compote

Preparation Time : 10 minutes
Cooking Time : 15 minutes
Servings : 6
Difficulty Level : Average

Ingredients:

- 1 cup apple juice
- 1 cup dry white wine
- 2 tablespoons honey
- 1 cinnamon stick
- ¼ teaspoon ground nutmeg
- 1 tablespoon grated lemon zest
- 1½ tablespoons grated orange zest
- 3 large apples, peeled, cored, and chopped
- 3 large pears, peeled, cored, and chopped
- ½ cup dried cherries

Directions:

Situate all ingredients in the Instant Pot® and stir well. Close and select the Manual button, and allow to sit for 1 minute. When the timer beeps, rapidly-release the pressure until the float valve hit the bottom. Click the Cancel then open lid.

Use a slotted spoon to transfer fruit to a serving bowl. Remove and discard cinnamon stick. Press the Sauté button and bring juice in the pot to a boil. Cook, stirring constantly, until reduced to a syrup that will coat the back of a spoon, about 10 minutes.

Stir syrup into fruit mixture. Once cool slightly, then wrap with plastic and chill overnight.

Nutrition (for 100g): 211 Calories 1g Fat 4g Carbohydrates 2g Protein 208mg Sodium

Stuffed Apples

Preparation Time : 10 minutes

Cooking Time : 15 minutes

Servings : 6

Difficulty Level : Difficult

Ingredients:

- ½ cup apple juice
- ¼ cup golden raisins
- ¼ cup chopped toasted walnuts
- 2 tablespoons sugar
- ½ teaspoon grated orange zest
- ½ teaspoon ground cinnamon
- 4 large cooking apples
- 4 teaspoons unsalted butter
- 1 cup water

Directions:

Put apple juice in a microwave-safe container; heat for 1 minute on high or until steaming and hot. Pour over raisins. Soak raisins for 30 minutes. Drain, reserving apple juice. Add nuts, sugar, orange zest, and cinnamon to raisins and stir to mix.

Cut off the top fourth of each apple. Peel the cut portion and chop it, then stir diced apple pieces into raisin mixture. Hollow out and core apples by cutting to, but not through, the bottoms.

Situate each apple on a piece of aluminum foil that is large enough to wrap apple completely. Fill apple centers with raisin mixture.

Top each with 1 teaspoon butter. Cover the foil around each apple, folding the foil over at the top and then pinching it firmly together.

Stir in water to the Instant Pot® and place rack inside. Place apples on the rack. Close lid, set steam release to Sealing, press the Manual, and alarm to 10 minutes.

When the timer beeps, quick-release the pressure until the float valve drops and open the lid. Carefully lift apples out of the Instant Pot®. Unwrap and transfer to plates. Serve hot, at room temperature, or cold.

Nutrition (for 100g): 432 Calories 16g Fat 6g Carbohydrates 3g Protein 361mg Sodium

Cinnamon-Stewed Dried Plums with Greek Yogurt

Preparation Time : 10 minutes

Cooking Time : 15 minutes

Servings : 6

Difficulty Level : Easy

Ingredients:

- 3 cups dried plums
- 2 cups water
- 2 tablespoons sugar
- 2 cinnamon sticks
- 3 cups low-fat plain Greek yogurt

Directions:

Add dried plums, water, sugar, and cinnamon to the Instant Pot®. Close allow steam release to Sealing, press the Manual button, and start the time to 3 minutes.

Once the timer beeps, quick-release the pressure. Click the Cancel button and open. Remove and discard cinnamon sticks. Serve warm over Greek yogurt.

Nutrition (for 100g): 301 Calories 2g Fat 3g Carbohydrates 14g Protein 244mg Sodium

Vanilla-Poached Apricots

Preparation Time : 10 minutes

Cooking Time : 20 minutes

Servings : 6

Difficulty Level : Average

Ingredients:

- 1¼ cups water
- ¼ cup marsala wine
- ¼ cup sugar
- 1 teaspoon vanilla bean paste
- 8 medium apricots, sliced in half and pitted

Directions:

Place all pieces in the Instant Pot® and combine well. Seal tight, click the Manual Instant Pot®. Stir to combine. Close lid, set steam release to Sealing, press the Manual button, and set second to 1 minute.

When the alarm beeps, quick-release the pressure until the float valve drops. Set the Cancel and open lid. Let stand for 10 minutes. Carefully remove apricots from poaching liquid with a slotted spoon. Serve warm or at room temperature.

Nutrition (for 100g): 62 Calories 1g Fat 5g Carbohydrates 2g Protein 311mg Sodium

Creamy Spiced Almond Milk

Preparation Time : 10 minutes

Cooking Time : 15 minutes

Servings : 6

Difficulty Level : Average

Ingredients:

- 1 cup raw almonds
- 5 cups filtered water, divided
- 1 teaspoon vanilla bean paste
- ½ teaspoon pumpkin pie spice

Directions:

Stir in almonds and 1 cup water to the Instant Pot®. Close and select the Manual, and set time to 1 minute.

When the timer alarms, quick-release the pressure until the float valve drops. Click the Cancel button and open cap. Strain almonds and rinse under cool water. Transfer to a high-powered blender with remaining 4 cups water. Purée for 2 minutes on high speed.

Incorporate mixture into a nut milk bag set over a large bowl. Squeeze bag to extract all liquid. Stir in vanilla and pumpkin pie spice. Transfer to a Mason jar or sealed jug and refrigerate for 8 hours. Stir or shake gently before serving.

Nutrition (for 100g): 86 Calories 8g Fat 5g Carbohydrates 3g Protein 259mg Sodium

Poached Pears with Greek Yogurt and Pistachio

Preparation Time: 10 minutes
Cooking Time: 15 minutes
Servings: 8
Difficulty Level: Average

Ingredients:

- 2 cups water
- 1¾ cups apple cider
- ¼ cup lemon juice
- 1 cinnamon stick
- 1 teaspoon vanilla bean paste
- 4 large Bartlett pears, peeled
- 1 cup low-fat plain Greek yogurt
- ½ cup unsalted roasted pistachio meats

Directions:

Add water, apple cider, lemon juice, cinnamon, vanilla, and pears to the Instant Pot®. Close lid, set steam release, switch the Manual, and set time to 3 minutes.

When the timer stops, swift-release the pressure until the float valve drops. Select the Cancel button and open cap. Take out pears to a plate and allow to cool to room temperature.

To serve, carefully slice pears in half with a sharp paring knife and scoop out core with a melon baller. Lay pear halves on dessert plates or in shallow bowls. Top with yogurt and garnish with pistachios. Serve immediately.

Nutrition (for 100g): 181 Calories 7g Fat 5g Carbohydrates 7g Protein 253mg Sodium

Peaches Poached in Rose Water

Preparation Time : 10 minutes

Cooking Time : 20 minutes

Servings : 6

Difficulty Level : Average

Ingredients:

- 1 cup water
- 1 cup rose water
- ¼ cup wildflower honey
- 8 green cardamom pods, lightly crushed
- 1 teaspoon vanilla bean paste
- 6 large yellow peaches, pitted and quartered
- ½ cup chopped unsalted roasted pistachio meats

Directions:

Add water, rose water, honey, cardamom, and vanilla to the Instant Pot®. Whisk well, then add peaches. Close lid, allow to steam release to Seal, press the Manual button, and alarm time to 1 minute.

When done, release the pressure until the float valve hits the bottom. Press the Remove and open it. Allow peaches to stand for 10 minutes. Carefully remove peaches from poaching liquid with a slotted spoon.

Slip skins from peach slices. Arrange slices on a plate and garnish with pistachios. Serve warm or at room temperature.

Nutrition (for 100g): 145 Calories 3g Fat 6g Carbohydrates 2g Protein 281mg Sodium

Brown Betty Apple Dessert

Preparation Time : 10 minutes

Cooking Time : 10 minutes

Servings :

Difficulty Level : Difficult

Ingredients:

- 2 cups dried bread crumbs
- ½ cup sugar
- 1 teaspoon ground cinnamon
- 3 tablespoons lemon juice
- 1 tablespoon grated lemon zest
- 1 cup olive oil, divided
- 8 medium apples, peeled, cored, and diced
- 2 cups water

Directions:

Combine crumbs, sugar, cinnamon, lemon juice, lemon zest, and ½ cup oil in a medium mixing bowl. Set aside.

In a greased oven-safe dish that will fit in your cooker loosely, add a thin layer of crumbs, then one diced apple. Continue filling the container with alternating layers of crumbs and apples until all ingredients are finished. Pour remaining ½ cup oil on top.

Pour water to the Instant Pot® and place rack inside. Make a foil sling by folding a long piece of foil in half lengthwise and lower the uncovered container into the pot using the sling.

Seal and press the Manual button, and set time to 10 minutes. When the timer stops, let pressure release naturally, about 20 minutes. Press the Cancel button and open lid. Using the sling, remove the baking dish from the pot and let stand for 5 minutes before serving.

Nutrition (for 100g): 422 Calories 27g Fat 4g Carbohydrates 7g Protein 355mg Sodium

Blueberry Oat Crumble

Preparation Time : 10 minutes

Cooking Time : 10 minutes

Servings : 8

Difficulty Level : Difficult

Ingredients:

- 1 cup water
- 4 cups blueberries
- 2 tablespoons packed light brown sugar
- 2 tablespoons cornstarch
- 1/8 teaspoon ground nutmeg
- 1/3 cup rolled oats
- ¼ cup granulated sugar
- ¼ cup all-purpose flour
- ¼ teaspoon ground cinnamon
- ¼ cup unsalted butter, melted and cooled

Directions:

Brush baking dish that fits inside the Instant Pot® with nonstick cooking spray. Add water to the pot and add rack. Crease a long piece of aluminum foil in half lengthwise. Lay foil over rack to form a sling.

In a medium bowl, combine blueberries, brown sugar, cornstarch, and nutmeg. Transfer mixture to prepared dish.

In a separate medium bowl, add oats, sugar, flour, and cinnamon. Mix well. Add butter and combine until mixture is crumbly. Sprinkle crumbles over blueberries, cover dish with aluminum foil, and crimp edges tightly.

Add baking dish to rack in pot so it rests on the sling and seal tight. Switch the Manual button, and set time to 10 minutes. When the timer beeps, let pressure release naturally for 10 minutes, then quick-release the remaining pressure until the float valve drops. Press the Cancel button and open lid. Carefully remove dish with sling and remove foil cover.

Heat broiler on high. Broil crumble until topping is golden brown, about 5 minutes. Serve warm or at room temperature.

Nutrition (for 100g): 159 Calories 6g Fat 3g Carbohydrates 2g Protein 477mg Sodium

Date and Walnut Cookies

Preparation Time : 10 minutes

Cooking Time : 2 minutes

Servings : 30

Difficulty Level : Average

Ingredients:

- 2 cups flour
- 1/4 cup sour cream
- 1/2 cup butter, softened
- 1 1/2 cups brown sugar
- 1/2 cup white sugar
- 1 egg
- 1 cup dates, pitted and chopped
- 1/3 cup water
- 1/4 cup walnuts, finely chopped
- 1/2 tsp salt
- 1/2 tsp baking soda
- a pinch of cinnamon

Directions:

Cook the dates together with the white sugar and water over medium-high heat, stirring constantly, until mixture is thick like jam. Add in the nuts, stir and remove from heat. Leave to cool.

In a medium bowl, scourge the butter and brown sugar. Stir in the egg and the sour cream. Mix the flour together with salt, baking soda and cinnamon and stir it into the butter mixture. Drop a teaspoon of dough onto a cookie sheet, place 1/4 teaspoon of the filling on top of it and top with an additional 1/2 teaspoon of dough. Repeat with the rest of the dough. Bake cookies for about 10 minutes in a preheated to 340 F oven, or until golden.

Nutrition (for 100g): 134 Calories 7.9g Fats 2g Carbohydrates 1.4g Protein 341mg Sodium

Moroccan Stuffed Dates

Preparation Time : 15 minutes

Cooking Time : 0 minutes

Servings : 30

Difficulty Level : Easy

Ingredients:

- 1 lb. dates
- 1 cup blanched almonds
- 1/4 cup sugar
- 1 1/2 tbsp orange flower water
- 1 tbsp butter, melted
- 1/4 teaspoon cinnamon

Directions:

Incorporate the almonds, sugar and cinnamon in a food processor. Stir in the butter and orange flower water and process until a smooth paste is formed. Roll small pieces of almond paste the same length as a date. Take one date, make a vertical cut and discard the pit. Insert a piece of the almond paste and press the sides of the date firmly around. Repeat with all the remaining dates and almond paste.

Nutrition (for 100g): 102 Calories 7g Fats 5g Carbohydrates 2g Protein 310mg Sodium

Fig Cookies

Preparation Time : 10 minutes

Cooking Time : 15 minutes

Servings : 24

Difficulty Level : Average

Ingredients:

- 1 cup flour
- 1 egg
- 1/2 cup sugar
- 1/2 cup figs, chopped
- 1/2 cup butter
- 1/4 cup water
- 1/2 tsp vanilla extract
- 1 tsp baking powder
- a pinch of salt

Directions:

Cook figs with water, stirring, for 4-5 minutes, or until thickened. Set aside to cool. Scourge butter with sugar until light and fluffy. Put in the egg and vanilla and beat to blend well. In separate bowl, incorporate together flour, baking powder and salt. Blend this into the egg mixture. Stir in the cooled figs.

Drop teaspoonfuls of dough on a greased baking tray. Bake in a preheated to 375 degrees F oven until lightly browned. Remove cookies and cool on wire racks.

Nutrition (for 100g): 111 Calories 9g Fats 5g Carbohydrates 3g Protein 253mg Sodium

Almond Cookies

Preparation Time : 10 minutes

Cooking Time : 15 minutes

Servings : 30

Difficulty Level : Easy

Ingredient:

- 1 cup almonds, blanched, toasted and finely chopped
- 1 cup powdered sugar
- 4 egg whites
- 2 tbsp flour
- 1/2 tsp vanilla extract
- 1 pinch ground cinnamon
- powdered sugar, to dust

Directions:

Preheat oven to 320 F. Blend the almonds in a food processor until finely chopped. Beat egg whites and sugar until thick. Add in vanilla extract and cinnamon. Gently stir in almonds and flour. Place tablespoonfuls of mixture on two lined baking trays. Bake for 10 minutes, or until firm. Turn it off, and leave cookies to cool. Dust with powdered sugar.

Nutrition (for 100g): 106 Calories 6g Fats 7g Carbohydrates 1g Protein 214mg Sodium

Turkish Delight Cookies

Preparation Time : 5 minutes

Cooking Time : 20 minutes

Servings : 48

Difficulty Level : Difficult

Ingredients:

- 4 cups flour
- 3/4 cup sugar
- 1 cup lard (or butter)
- 3 eggs
- 1 tsp baking powder
- 1 tsp vanilla extract
- 8 oz Turkish delight, chopped
- powdered sugar, for dusting

Directions:

Ready oven to 375 F. Put parchment paper onto the baking sheet. Beat the eggs well, adding sugar a bit at a time. Beat for at least 3 minutes. Melt the lard, then let it cool enough and slowly combine it with the egg mixture.

Mix the flour and the baking powder. Lightly add the flour mixture to the egg and lard mixture to create a smooth dough. Divide dough into two or three smaller balls and roll it out until ¼ inch thick. Cut squares 3x2 inch. Situate a piece of Turkish delight in each square, roll each cookie into a stick and nip the end. Bake in a preheated to 350 degrees F oven until light pink. Dust in powdered sugar and store in an airtight container when completely cool.

Nutrition (for 100g): 109 Calories 7g Fats 5g Carbohydrates 3g Protein 205mg Sodium

Anise Cookies

Preparation Time : 10 minutes

Cooking Time : 20 minutes

Servings : 24

Difficulty Level : Average

Ingredients:

- 1 ½ cups flour
- 1/3 cup sugar
- 1/3 cup olive oil
- 1 egg, whisked
- 3 tsp fennel seeds
- 1 tsp cinnamon
- zest of one orange
- 3 tbsp anise liqueur
- sugar, for sprinkling

Directions:

Cook olive oil in a small pan and sauté fennel seeds for 20-30 seconds. In a large bowl, combine together flour, sugar, and cinnamon. Add in olive oil, stirring, until well combined. Add orange zest and anise liqueur. Mix well then knead with hands until a smooth dough is formed. Add a little water if necessary.

On a well-floured surface, form two 1-inch long logs. Cut 1/8-inch cookies, arrange them on greased baking sheets. Egg wash each cookie and sprinkle with sugar. Bake cookies in a preheated to 350 F oven, for about 10 minutes, or until golden and crisp. Once cool, put in an airtight container.

Nutrition (for 100g): 113 Calories 8g Fats 5g Carbohydrates 2g Protein 255mg Sodium

Spanish Nougat

Preparation Time : 5 minutes

Cooking Time : 20 minutes

Servings : 24

Difficulty Level : Average

Ingredients:

- 1 1/2 cup honey
- 3 egg whites
- 1 ¾ cup almonds, roasted and chopped

Directions:

Put the honey into a saucepan and boil over medium-high heat, then set aside to cool. Beat the egg whites to a thick glossy meringue and fold them into the honey. Bring the mixture back to medium-high heat and let it simmer, constantly stirring, for 15 minutes. When the color and consistency change to dark caramel, remove from heat, add the almonds and mix trough.

Put foil in a 9x13 inch pan and pour the hot mixture on it. Cover with another piece of foil and even out. Let cool completely. Place a wooden board weighted down with some heavy cans on it. Leave like this for 3-4 days, so it hardens and dries out. Slice into 1-inch squares.

Nutrition (for 100g): 110 Calories 5g Fats 7g Carbohydrates 1g Protein 336mg Sodium

Spanish Crumble Cakes

Preparation Time : 10 minutes

Cooking Time : 25 minutes

Servings : 30

Difficulty Level : Difficult

Ingredients:

- 2 cups flour
- 1 cup butter, softened
- 1 cup sugar
- 1 egg
- 1 tsp lemon zest
- 1 tsp orange zest
- 1 tbsp orange juice
- 1/2 cup almonds, blanched and finely ground

Directions:

Beat butter with sugar, lemon and orange zest until light. Combine in the flour, using a wooden spoon. Add ground almonds, stir, then knead with your hands until dough clings together. Divide it in three parts. Seal and chill for at least half an hour.

On a well-floured surface, roll out each piece of dough until it is 1/4 inch thick. Cut into different shapes. Arrange cookies on an ungreased baking sheet.

Beat together egg and orange juice and brush this over the cookies. Bake in a preheated to 350 degrees F oven for 7-8 minutes, or until edges are lightly golden. Set aside and keep in an airtight container.

Nutrition (for 100g): 113 Calories 8g Fats 5g Carbohydrates 4g Protein 204mg Sodium

Greek Honey Cookies

Preparation Time : 10 minutes

Cooking Time : 15 minutes

Servings : 40

Difficulty Level : Difficult

Ingredients:

- 1 ¾ cups olive oil
- 2 cups walnuts, coarsely ground
- 1 cup sugar
- 1 cup fresh orange juice
- 3 tbsp orange peel
- 1/3 cup cognac
- 1 ½ tsp baking soda
- 1 tsp baking powder
- sifted flour, enough to make soft oily dough
- for the syrup
- 2 cups honey
- 1 cup water
- for sprinkling
- 1 cup very finely ground walnuts
- 1 tsp ground cinnamon
- 1 tsp ground cloves

Directions:

Line 2 baking trays with baking paper. In a very large bowl, scourge together oil, sugar, orange zest, orange juice, cognac, baking soda, baking powder, and salt until well combined. Fold in flour with a wooden spoon until a soft dough is formed.

Roll tablespoonfuls of the mixture into balls. Place them, about 1.5 inch apart, on the prepared trays. With a fork to prick the top of each cookie by cross-pressing. Bake in a preheated to 350 degrees F oven, for 30-35 minutes, or until golden.

Situate the water and honey in a medium saucepan over medium-high heat. Simmer for 5 minutes, removing foam. Lower heat and with the help of a perforated spoon, dip 5-6 cookies at a time into the syrup. Once the cookies have absorbed a little of the syrup, remove them with the same spoon and situate them on a tray to cool and get rid of any excess syrup. After dipping the cookies, sprinkle with a mixture of cinnamon, cloves and finely ground walnuts.

Nutrition (for 100g): 116 Calories 7g Fats 6g Carbohydrates 2g Protein 241mg Sodium

Cinnamon Butter Cookies

Preparation Time : 10 minutes

Cooking Time : 20 minutes

Servings : 24

Difficulty Level : Average

Ingredients:

- 2 cups flour
- 1/2 cup sugar
- 5 tbsp butter
- 3 eggs
- 1 tbsp cinnamon

Directions:

Scourge the butter and sugar until light and fluffy. Combine the flour and the cinnamon. Beat eggs into the butter mixture. Gently add in the flour. Situate the dough onto a lightly floured surface and knead just once or twice until smooth.

Form a roll and divide it into 24 pieces. Grease and line baking sheets with parchment paper. Spread each piece of cookie dough into a long thin strip, then make a circle, flatten a little and set it on the prepared baking sheet. Bake cookies, in batches, in a preheated to 350 F oven, for 12 to 15 minutes. Set aside in a cooling rack.

Nutrition (for 100g): 111 Calories 5g Fats 3g Carbohydrates 9g Protein 230mg Sodium

Best French Meringues

Preparation Time : 10 minutes

Cooking Time : 2 hours and 30 minutes

Servings : 36

Difficulty Level : Average

Ingredients:

- 4 egg whites
- 2 1/4 cups powdered sugar

Directions:

Ready the oven to 200 F and line a baking sheet.

In a glass bowl, beat egg whites with an electric mixer. Mix in sugar a little simultaneously, while continuing to beat at medium speed. When the egg white mixture becomes stiff and shiny like satin, transfer to a large pastry bag. Place the meringue onto the lined baking sheet with the use of a large round.

Put the meringues in the oven and leave the oven door slightly ajar. Bake until the meringues are dry.

Nutrition (for 100g): 110 Calories 11g Fat 6g Carbohydrates 3g Protein 230mg Sodium

Cinnamon Palmier

Preparation Time : 5 minutes

Cooking Time : 15 minutes

Servings : 30

Difficulty Level : Easy

Ingredients:

- 1/3 cup granulated sugar
- 2 tsp cinnamon
- 1/2 lb. puff pastry
- 1 egg, beaten (optional)

Directions:

Stir together the sugar and cinnamon. Spread the pastry dough into a large rectangle. Spread the cinnamon sugar in an even layer over the dough. From the long ends of the rectangle, loosely roll each side inward until they meet in the middle. If needed, brush it with the egg to hold it together. Slice the pastry roll crosswise into 1/4-inch pieces and arrange them on a lined with parchment paper baking sheet. Bake cookies in a preheated to 400 F oven for 12-15 minutes, until they puff and turn golden brown. Serve warm or at room temperature.

Nutrition (for 100g): 114 Calories 3g Fats 8g Carbohydrates 6g Protein 274mg Sodium

Honey Sesame Cookies

Preparation Time : 10 minutes

Cooking Time : 15 minutes

Servings : 30

Difficulty Level : Difficult

Ingredients:

- 3 cups flour
- 1 cup sugar
- 1 cup butter
- 2 eggs
- 3 tbsp honey
- 1 cup pistachio nuts, roughly chopped
- 1 cup sesame seeds
- 1 tbsp vinegar
- 1 tsp vanilla
- 1 tsp baking powder
- a pinch of salt

Directions:

Scourge the butter and the sugar until light and fluffy. Gently add in the eggs, then the vanilla extract and the vinegar. Incorporate the flour, salt, and baking powder and stir in the butter mixture. Beat until just incorporated. Cover and refrigerate for an hour.

Mix the sesame seeds and the honey in a medium plate. Place the pistachios in another one. Take a teaspoonful of dough, form it into a ball, then dip it into the pistachios. Press a little and dip it into the sesame-honey mixture. Repeat with the remaining dough, arranging the cookies on a lined baking sheet.

Bake the cookies in a preheated to 350 F oven for 15 minutes, or until they turn light brown. Set aside in the baking sheet for 2-3 minutes then move to a wire rack.

Nutrition (for 100g): 117 Calories 9g Fats 7g Carbohydrates 1g Protein 214mg Sodium

Baked Apples

Preparation Time : 5 minutes

Cooking Time : 10 minutes

Servings : 4

Difficulty Level : Easy

Ingredients:

- 8 medium sized apples
- 1/3 cup walnuts, crushed
- 3/4 cup sugar
- 3 tbsp raisins, soaked in brandy or dark rum
- vanilla, cinnamon according to taste
- 2 oz butter

Directions:

Peel and carefully hollow the apples. Prepare stuffing by beating the butter, 3/4 cup of sugar, crushed walnuts, raisins and cinnamon. Fill in the apples with this mixture and situate them in an oiled dish. Sprinkle the apples with 1-2 tablespoons of water and bake in a moderate oven. Serve warm and side it with vanilla ice cream.

Nutrition (for 100g): 107 Calories 9g Fats 7g Carbohydrates 3g Protein 236mg Sodium

Pumpkin Baked with Dry Fruit

Preparation Time : 10 minutes

Cooking Time : 15 minutes

Servings : 6

Difficulty Level : Easy

Ingredients:

- 1.5 lb. pumpkin, cut into medium pieces
- 1 cup dry fruit (apricots, plums, apples, raisins)
- 1/2 cup brown sugar

Directions:

Soak the dry fruit in some water, drain and discard the water. Cut the pumpkin in medium cubes. At the bottom of a pot arrange a layer of pumpkin pieces, then a layer of dry fruit and then again, some pumpkin. Add a little water. Cover the pot and bring to boil. Simmer until there is no more water. When almost ready add the sugar. Serve warm or cold.

Nutrition (for 100g): 113 Calories 8g Fats 5g Carbohydrates 3g Protein 311mg Sodium

Banana Shake Bowls

Preparation Time : 5 minutes

Cooking Time : 0 minutes

Servings : 4

Difficulty Level : Easy

Ingredients:

- 4 medium bananas, peeled
- 1 avocado, peeled, pitted and mashed
- ¾ cup almond milk
- ½ teaspoon vanilla extract

Directions:

In a blender, meld the bananas with the avocado and the other ingredients, pulse, divide into bowls and store in the fridge until serving.

Nutrition (for 100g): 185 Calories 4.3g Fat 6g Carbohydrates 6.45g Protein 214mg Sodium

Cold Lemon Squares

Preparation Time : 30 minutes

Cooking Time : 0 minutes

Servings : 4

Difficulty Level : Easy

Ingredients:

- 1 cup avocado oil+ a drizzle
- 2 bananas, peeled and chopped
- 1 tablespoon honey
- ¼ cup lemon juice
- A pinch of lemon zest, grated

Directions:

In your food processor, mix the bananas with the rest of the ingredients, pulse well and spread on the bottom of a pan greased with a drizzle of oil. Introduce in the fridge for 30 minutes, slice into squares and serve.

Nutrition (for 100g): 136 Calories 11.2g Fat 7g Carbohydrates 1.1g Protein 236mg Sodium

Blackberry and Apples Cobbler

Preparation Time : 10 minutes

Cooking Time : 30 minutes

Servings : 6

Difficulty Level : Average

Ingredients:

- ¾ cup stevia
- 6 cups blackberries
- ¼ cup apples, cored and cubed
- ¼ teaspoon baking powder
- 1 tablespoon lime juice
- ½ cup almond flour
- ½ cup water
- 3 and ½ tablespoon avocado oil
- Cooking spray

Directions:

In a bowl, combine the berries with half of the stevia and lemon juice, sprinkle some flour all over, whisk and pour into a baking dish greased with cooking spray.

In another bowl, mix flour with the rest of the sugar, baking powder, the water and the oil, and stir the whole thing with your hands. Spread over the berries, introduce in the oven at 375 degrees F and bake for 30 minutes.

Serve warm.

Nutrition (for 100g): 221 Calories 6.3g Fat 6g Carbohydrates 9g Protein 350mg Sodium

Black Tea Cake

Preparation Time : 10 minutes

Cooking Time : 35 minutes

Servings : 8

Difficulty Level : Average

Ingredients:

- 6 tablespoons black tea powder
- 2 cups almond milk, warmed up
- 1 cup avocado oil
- 2 cups stevia
- 4 eggs
- 2 teaspoons vanilla extract
- 3 and ½ cups almond flour
- 1 teaspoon baking soda
- 3 teaspoons baking powder

Directions:

Stir well the almond milk with the oil, stevia and the rest of the ingredients. Pour this into a cake pan lined with parchment paper, introduce in the oven at 350 degrees F and bake for 35 minutes. Leave the cake to cool down, slice and serve.

Nutrition (for 100g): 200 Calories 6.4g Fat 6.5g Carbohydrates 5.4g Protein 384mg Sodium

Green Tea and Vanilla Cream

Preparation Time : 2 hours
Cooking Time : 0 minutes
Servings : 4
Difficulty Level : Easy

Ingredients:

- 14 ounces almond milk, hot
- 2 tablespoons green tea powder
- 14 ounces heavy cream
- 3 tablespoons stevia
- 1 teaspoon vanilla extract
- 1 teaspoon gelatin powder

Directions:

Incorporate well the almond milk with the green tea powder and the rest of the ingredients, cool down, divide into cups and keep in the fridge for 2 hours before serving.

Nutrition (for 100g): 120 Calories 3g Fat 7g Carbohydrates 4g Protein 293mg Sodium

Figs Pie

Preparation Time : 10 minutes

Cooking Time : 60 minutes

Servings : 8

Difficulty Level : Average

Ingredients:

- ½ cup stevia
- 6 figs, cut into quarters
- ½ teaspoon vanilla extract
- 1 cup almond flour
- 4 eggs, whisked

Directions:

Spread the figs on the bottom of a springform pan lined with parchment paper. In a bowl, combine the other ingredients, whisk and pour over the figs. Bake at 375 digress F for 1 hour, flip the pie upside down when it's done and serve.

Nutrition (for 100g): 200 Calories 4.4g Fat 7.6g Carbohydrates 8g Protein 351mg Sodium

Cherry Cream

Preparation Time : 2 hours
Cooking Time : 0 minutes
Servings : 4
Difficulty Level : Easy

Ingredients:

- 2 cups cherries, pitted and chopped
- 1 cup almond milk
- ½ cup whipping cream
- 3 eggs, whisked
- 1/3 cup stevia
- 1 teaspoon lemon juice
- ½ teaspoon vanilla extract

Directions:

In your food processor, combine the cherries with the milk and the rest of the ingredients, pulse well, divide into cups and keep in the fridge for 2 hours before serving.

Nutrition (for 100g): 200 Calories 4.5g Fat 5.6g Carbohydrates 3.4g Protein 278mg Sodium

Strawberries Cream

Preparation Time : 10 minutes

Cooking Time : 20 minutes

Servings : 4

Difficulty Level : Easy

Ingredients:

- ½ cup stevia
- 2 pounds strawberries, chopped
- 1 cup almond milk
- Zest of 1 lemon, grated
- ½ cup heavy cream
- 3 egg yolks, whisked

Directions:

Heat up a pan with the milk over medium-high heat, add the stevia and the rest of the ingredients, whisk well, simmer for 20 minutes, divide into cups and serve cold.

Nutrition (for 100g): 152 Calories 4.4g Fat 5.1g Carbohydrates 0.8g Protein 361mg Sodium

Apples and Plum Cake

Preparation Time : 10 minutes

Cooking Time : 40 minutes

Servings : 4

Difficulty Level : Average

Ingredients:

- 7 ounces almond flour
- 1 egg, whisked
- 5 tablespoons stevia
- 3 ounces warm almond milk
- 2 pounds plums, pitted and cut into quarters
- 2 apples, cored and chopped
- Zest of 1 lemon, grated
- 1 tsp baking powder

Directions:

Blend well the almond milk with the egg, stevia, and the rest of the ingredients except the cooking spray

Grease a cake pan with the oil, pour the cake mix inside, introduce in the oven at 350 degrees F for 40 minutes.

Cool down, slice and serve.

Nutrition (for 100g): 209 Calories 6.4g Fat 8g Carbohydrates 6.6g Protein 281mg Sodium

Cinnamon Chickpeas Cookies

Preparation Time : 10 minutes

Cooking Time : 20 minutes

Servings : 12

Difficulty Level : Average

Ingredients:

- 1 cup canned chickpeas
- 2 cups almond flour
- 1 teaspoon cinnamon powder
- 1 teaspoon baking powder
- 1 cup avocado oil
- ½ cup stevia
- 1 egg, whisked
- 2 teaspoons almond extract
- 1 cup raisins
- 1 cup coconut, unsweetened and shredded

Directions:

In a bowl, combine the chickpeas with the flour, cinnamon and the other ingredients, and whisk well until you obtain a dough.

Scoop tablespoons of dough on a baking sheet lined with parchment paper, introduce in oven for 20 minutes at 350 degrees. Let it cool and serve.

Nutrition (for 100g): 200 Calories 4.5g Fat 9.5g Carbohydrates 2.4g Protein 311mg Sodium

Cocoa Brownies

Preparation Time : 10 minutes
Cooking Time : 20 minutes
Servings : 8
Difficulty Level : Average

Ingredients:

- 30 ounces canned lentils, rinsed and drained
- 1 tablespoon honey
- 1 banana, peeled and chopped
- ½ teaspoon baking soda
- 4 tablespoons almond butter
- 2 tablespoons cocoa powder
- Cooking spray

Directions:

In a food processor, pulse well the lentils with the honey and the other ingredients except the cooking spray.

Transfer this into a pan greased with cooking spray, lay evenly, introduce in the oven at 375 degrees F for 20 minutes. Slice the brownies and serve cold.

Nutrition (for 100g): 200 Calories 4.5g Fat 8.7g Carbohydrates 4.3g Protein 252mg Sodium

Cardamom Almond Cream

Preparation Time : 30 minutes

Cooking Time : 0 minutes

Servings : 4

Difficulty Level : Easy

Ingredients:

- Juice of 1 lime
- ½ cup stevia
- 1 and ½ cups water
- 3 cups almond milk
- ½ cup honey
- 2 teaspoons cardamom, ground
- 1 teaspoon rose water
- 1 teaspoon vanilla extract

Directions:

In a blender, blend well the almond milk with the cardamom and the rest of the ingredients, divide into cups and keep in the fridge for 30 minutes before serving.

Nutrition (for 100g): 283 Calories 11.8g Fat 4.7g Carbohydrates 7.1g Protein 321mg Sodium

Banana Cinnamon Cupcakes

Preparation Time : 10 minutes

Cooking Time : 20 minutes

Servings : 4

Difficulty Level : Easy

Ingredients :

- 4 tablespoons avocado oil
- 4 eggs
- ½ cup orange juice
- 2 teaspoons cinnamon powder
- 1 teaspoon vanilla extract
- 2 bananas, peeled and chopped
- ¾ cup almond flour
- ½ teaspoon baking powder
- Cooking spray

Directions:

In a bowl, combine the oil with the eggs, orange juice and the other ingredients except the cooking spray, whisk well, pour in a cupcake pan greased with the cooking spray. Introduce in oven for 20 minutes, at 350 degrees F.

Cool the cupcakes down and serve.

Nutrition (for 100g): 142 Calories 5.8g Fat 5.7g Carbohydrates 1.6g Protein 214mg Sodium

Rhubarb and Apples Cream

Preparation Time : 10 minutes

Cooking Time : 0 minutes

Servings : 6

Difficulty Level : Easy

Ingredients:

- 3 cups rhubarb, chopped
- 1 and ½ cups stevia
- 2 eggs, whisked
- ½ teaspoon nutmeg, ground
- 1 tablespoon avocado oil
- 1/3 cup almond milk

Directions:

In a blender, combine the rhubarb with the stevia and the rest of the ingredients, pulse well, divide into cups and serve cold.

Nutrition (for 100g): 200 Calories 5.2g Fat 7.6g Carbohydrates 2.5g Protein

Almond Rice Dessert

Preparation Time : 10 minutes
Cooking Time : 20 minutes
Servings : 4
Difficulty Level : Easy

Ingredients:

- 1 cup white rice
- 2 cups almond milk
- 1 cup almonds, chopped
- ½ cup stevia
- 1 tablespoon cinnamon powder
- ½ cup pomegranate seeds

Directions:

In a pot, incorporate the rice with the milk and stevia, bring to a simmer and cook for 20 minutes, stirring often. Add the rest of the ingredients, stir, divide into bowls and serve.

Nutrition (for 100g): 234 Calories 9.5g Fat 12.4g Carbohydrates 6.5g Protein 317mg Sodium

Mediterranean Baked Apples

Preparation Time : 5 minutes

Cooking Time : 25 minutes

Servings : 4

Difficulty Level : Easy

Ingredients:

- 1.5 pounds apples, peeled and sliced
- Juice from ½ lemon
- A dash of cinnamon

Directions:

Preheat the oven to 2500 F. Line a baking sheet with parchment paper then set aside. In a medium bowl, apples with lemon juice and cinnamon. Place the apples on the parchment paper-lined baking sheet. Bake for 25 minutes until crisp.

Nutrition (for 100g): 90 Calories 0.3g Fat 23.9g Carbohydrates 0.5g Protein 633mg Sodium

Chia Almond Butter Pudding

Preparation Time : 5 minutes

Cooking Time : 10 minutes

Servings : 1

Difficulty Level : Easy

Ingredients:

- ¼ cup chia seeds
- 1 cup unsweetened almond milk
- 1 ½ tablespoons maple syrup
- 2 ½ tablespoons almond butter

Directions:

Add almond milk, maple syrup, and almond butter in a bowl and stir well. Add chia seeds and stir to mix. Pour pudding mixture into the Mason jar and place it in the refrigerator overnight. Serve and enjoy.

Nutrition (for 100g): 354 Calories 21.3g Fat 31.1g Carbohydrates 11.2g Protein 251mg Sodium

Sweet Rice Pudding

Preparation Time : 10 minutes

Cooking Time : 30 minutes

Servings : 4

Difficulty Level : Average

Ingredients:

- 1 ¼ cup of rice
- ¼ cup dark chocolate, chopped
- 1 teaspoon vanilla
- 1/3 cup coconut butter
- 1 teaspoon liquid stevia
- 2 ½ cup almond milk

Directions:

Incorporate all ingredients inside the inner pot and mix well. Cover and cook on high for 20 minutes. Once done, allow to release pressure naturally. Remove lid. Stir well and serve.

Nutrition (for 100g): 638 Calories 39.9g Fat 63.5g Carbohydrates 8.6g Protein 354mg Sodium

Creamy Yogurt Banana Bowls

Preparation Time : 15 minutes

Cooking Time : 0 minutes

Servings : 4

Difficulty Level : Easy

Ingredients:

- 2 bananas, sliced
- ½ teaspoon ground nutmeg
- 3 tablespoon flaxseed meal
- ¼ cup creamy peanut butter
- 4 cups Greek yogurt

Directions:

Divide Greek yogurt between 4 serving bowls and top with sliced bananas. Add peanut butter in microwave-safe bowl and microwave for 30 seconds.

Drizzle 1 tablespoon of melted peanut butter on each bowl on top of the sliced bananas. Sprinkle cinnamon and flax meal on top and serve.

Nutrition (for 100g): 351 Calories 13.1g Fat 35.6g Carbohydrates 19.6g Protein 322mg Sodium

. Lemon Pear Compote

Preparation Time : 5 minutes

Cooking Time : 15 minutes

Servings : 6

Difficulty Level : Average

Ingredients:

- 3 cups pears, cored and cut into chunks
- 1 teaspoon vanilla
- 1 teaspoon liquid stevia
- 1 tablespoon lemon zest, grated
- 2 tablespoons lemon juice

Directions:

Stir all ingredients into the instant pot well. Cover and cook on high for 15 minutes. Once finished, release pressure naturally for 10 minutes then releases the remaining using quick release. Remove lid. Stir and serve.

Nutrition (for 100g): 50 Calories 0.2g Fat 12.7g Carbohydrates 0.4g Protein 310mg Sodium

Healthy & Quick Energy Bites

Preparation Time : 60 minutes

Cooking Time : 0 minutes

Servings : 20

Difficulty Level : Easy

Ingredients:

- 2 cups cashew nuts
- ¼ teaspoon cinnamon
- 1 teaspoon lemon zest
- 4 tablespoons dates, chopped
- 1/3 cup unsweetened shredded coconut
- ¾ cup dried apricots

Directions:

Put parchment paper into the baking sheet and set aside. Add all ingredients in a food processor and process until the mixture is crumbly and well combined. Make small balls from mixture and place on a prepared baking tray. Place in refrigerator for 1 hour. Serve and enjoy.

Nutrition (for 100g): 100 Calories 7.5g Fat 7.2g Carbohydrates 2.4g Protein 203mg Sodium

Healthy Coconut Blueberry Balls

Preparation Time : 60 minutes

Cooking Time : 5 minutes

Servings : 12

Difficulty Level : Easy

Ingredients:

- ¼ cup flaked coconut
- ¼ cup blueberries
- ½ teaspoon vanilla
- ¼ cup honey
- ½ cup creamy almond butter
- ¼ teaspoon cinnamon
- 1 ½ tablespoon chia seeds
- ¼ cup flaxseed meal
- 1 cup rolled oats, gluten-free

Directions:

In a large bowl, add oats, cinnamon, chia seeds, and flaxseed meal and mix well. Add almond butter in microwave-safe bowl and microwave for 30 seconds. Stir until smooth. Add vanilla and honey in melted almond butter and stir well.

Incorporate almond butter mixture over oat mixture and mix. Add coconut and blueberries and stir well. Make small balls from oat mixture and place onto the baking tray and place in the refrigerator for 1 hour. Serve and enjoy.

Nutrition (for 100g): 129 Calories 7.4g Fat 14.1g Carbohydrates 7g Protein 321mg Sodium

Panna Cotta

Preparation Time : 5 minutes

Cooking Time : 10 minutes + 4 hours

Servings : 2

Difficulty Level : Average

Ingredients:

- 1/3 cup skim milk
- 1 (0.25-ounce) envelope unflavored gelatin
- 2½ cups heavy cream
- ½ cup white sugar
- 1½ tsps. vanilla extract
- 1/3 cup red berries for decoration

Directions:

Place milk into a small bowl and stir in the envelope of gelatin. Set aside. Add the heavy cream and sugar to a saucepan, stirring, and set over medium-low heat. Watching carefully, let it come to a full boil.

Pour the gelatin-milk mixture into the cream, stirring until completely dissolved. Cook for one minute, stirring. Take away from heat, stir in the vanilla extract and pour into six ramekin dishes.

Allow to cool to room temperature. Before serving, cover with plastic wrap and freeze for at least 4 hours, but preferably overnight. Top with red berries before serving.

Nutrition (for 100g): 105 Calories 9g Fat 6g Carbohydrates 1g Protein 324mg Sodium

Turkish Kunefe

Preparation Time : 10 minutes

Cooking Time : 55 minutes

Servings : 2

Difficulty Level : Difficult

Ingredients:

- <u>For syrup:</u>
- 1 cup sugar
- 1 slice of lemon
- 1 cup water
- <u>For kunefe:</u>
- ½ cup butter melted to room temperature
- 1 tbsp butter for pans
- 2 cups shredded raw kadaifi dough
- ½ cup unsalted melting cheese of your choice
- 1 tbsp ground pistachios

Directions:

In a pot, add all syrup ingredients.

Let it boil, then adjust heat and simmer for 15 minutes until it gets a little thicker. Allow to cool.

Preheat the stove to 400° F. Put kadaifi dough to a bowl and coat with ½ cup melted butter. Lightly brush the bottom of four 9-inch pans with melted butter.

Divide the half of the dough in two pans evenly. Press it with your hand. Sprinkle noodles with cheese evenly. Press with your hand.

Cover with the remaining kadaifi dough and press it with your hand. Put to oven and bake for 10-15 minutes or until the top is golden-brown.

Turn each of two extra pans over, carefully place it above the dessert and flip the dessert into that extra pan. Now golden-brown side is on the bottom. Put it back to oven and bake for 10-15 minutes more or until the top side is golden-brown as well.

As soon as you remove dessert from the stove, pour syrup over them. Allow syrup to absorb and serve immediately while it's still hot, topping with ground pistachios.

Nutrition (for 100g): 508 Calories 25g Fat 57g Carbohydrates 19g Protein 226mg Sodium

Crema Catalana

Preparation Time : 3 hours
Cooking Time : 10 minutes
Servings : 2
Difficulty Level : Average

Ingredients:

- 4 large egg yolks
- 1 cup sugar
- 1 cinnamon stick
- Zest of 1 lemon
- 2 cups whole milk
- 1 Tbsp cornstarch

Directions:

Whisk ¾ cup sugar and the egg yolks in a large saucepan until the ingredients are thoroughly mixed and the mixture becomes frothy.

Add the lemon zest and cinnamon stick.

Add the cornstarch and milk and heat the mixture slowly, stirring constantly, just until it begins to thicken. Remove the pot from the heat immediately.

Pull out the cinnamon stick and fill the mixture into 2 ramekins to cool.

Cool to room temperature, then freeze for at least 2-3 hours.

Before serving, heat the broiler. Sprinkle the sugar over each ramekin. Place the ramekins under the broiler and let the sugar caramelize, bubble, and turn golden brown, about 5-10 minutes. Remove and serve immediately.

Nutrition (for 100g): 372 Calories 10g Fat 61g Carbohydrates 12g Protein 305mg Sodium

Spanish Dessert Turron

Preparation Time : 15 minutes

Cooking Time : 15 minutes

Servings : 2

Difficulty Level : Average

Ingredients:

- 1 cup baked almond
- 100 g honey
- 100 g sugar
- 2 pieces egg white
- 1-piece waffles
- 1 cup hazelnut

Directions:

Add nuts in a blender and chop for 10-15 seconds. Keep large pieces.

Cover baking form using a waffle paper.

Combine sugar and honey in a saucepan and melt on low heat.

Whisk egg whites. Combine nuts with egg whites and stir gently. Add nut paste to honey mix and cook for 10 minutes more on very low heat. It should have a light caramel color.

Spread it evenly onto the baking form. Let it chill in a cold place, and NOT IN THE FRIDGE.

Nutrition (for 100g): 216 Calories 14g Fat 16g Carbohydrates 6g Protein 230mg Sodium

Shrimp & Pasta

Preparation Time : 10 minutes

Cooking Time : 10 minutes

Servings : 2

Difficulty Level : Average

Ingredients:

- 2 Cups Angel Hair Pasta, Cooked
- 1/2 lb. Medium Shrimp, Peeled
- 1 Clove Garlic, Minced
- 1 Cup Tomato, Chopped
- 1 Teaspoon Olive Oil
- 1/6 Cup Kalamata Olives, Pitted & Chopped
- 1/8 Cup Basil, Fresh & Sliced Thin
- 1 Tablespoon Capers, Drained
- 1/8 Cup Feta Cheese, Crumbled
- Dash Black Pepper

Directions:

Cook your pasta per package instructions, and then heat your olive oil in a skillet using medium-high heat. Cook your garlic for half a minute, and then add your shrimp. Sauté for a minute more.

Add your basil and tomato, and then reduce the heat to allow it to simmer for three minutes. Your tomato should be tender.

Stir in your olives and capers. Add a dash of black pepper, and combine your shrimp mix and pasta to serve. Top with cheese before serving warm.

Nutrition (for 100g): 357 calories 11g fats 9g carbohydrates 30g protein 871mg sodium

Poached Cod

Preparation Time : 10 minutes

Cooking Time : 25 minutes

Servings : 2

Difficulty Level : Average

Ingredients:

- 2 Cod Filets, 6 Ounces
- Sea Salt & Black Pepper to Taste
- 1/4 Cup Dry White Wine
- 1/4 Cup Seafood Stock
- 2 Cloves Garlic, Minced
- 1 Bay Leaf
- 1/2 Teaspoon Sage, Fresh & Chopped
- 2 Rosemary Sprigs to Garnish

Directions:

Start by turning your oven to 375, and then season the fillets with salt and pepper. Place them in a baking pan, and add in your stock, garlic, wine, sage and bay leaf. Cover well, and then bake for twenty minutes. Your fish should be flaky when tested with a fork.

Use a spatula to remove each fillet, placing the liquid over high heat and cooking to reduce in half. This should take ten minutes, and you need to stir frequently. Serve dripped in poaching liquid and garnished with a rosemary sprig.

Nutrition (for 100g): 361 calories 10g fats 9g carbohydrates 34g protein 783mg sodium

www.ingramcontent.com/pod-product-compliance
Lightning Source LLC
Chambersburg PA
CBHW071818080526
44589CB00012B/838